Crossing the Centuries, Committed to Care

Crossing the Centuries, Committed to Care

BLUE CROSS AND BLUE SHIELD IN NORTH CAROLINA, 1933–2008

Diana J. Newton

Blue Cross and Blue Shield of North Carolina, Chapel Hill, North Carolina

Design and production by Chris Crochetière,
BW&A Books, Inc.,
Durham, North Carolina

Blue Cross and Blue Shield of North Carolina is an independent
licensee of the Blue Cross and Blue Shield Association.

Contents

Acknowledgments

As soon as I began doing research for this book, it became clear that it was going to be about much more than the story of one health insurance company in one state. Understanding medical advances and health insurance trends in the state and nation over the past 75 years led me down research paths I never expected and through more than 40 interviews, all of which were rich and illuminating in their distinctive way. I am deeply grateful to the many people who spent time and energy sharing with me their memories, their old photos, and their perspectives on Blue Cross and Blue Shield of North Carolina's remarkable development and long-standing commitment to the health of its members and the people of this state.

A book like this begins with those who value the power of history in helping us understand our past, appreciate our present, and shape our future. Thanks to Brad Wilson of BCBSNC for sponsoring this project and engaging Dr. Steven Channing of Video Dialog Inc. to make it happen.

Much of the "inside" story of BCBSNC came from extensive interviews with numerous former and current BCBSNC members of the Board of Trustees, executives, and employees, including: Brad Adcock, Don Bradley, Valerie Carter, Mary Chadwick, Willie Mae Ellison, Shirley Frye, Barbara Geer, Bob Greczyn, Ann Hamilton, Kathy Higgins, Bill Houck, Malissa Lee, Ken Lerner, Sara and Wayne Lindley, Harold Martin, John McClam, Alex McMahon, Bill Moffatt, Virginia Nunn, Catherine Oldham, Ken Otis, Betsy Parker, Howard Penton, Harry Reynolds, John Roos, Tom Rose, Rhone Sasser, Bernice Wade, Leo Waggoner, Margaret Watts, Gerald White, and Brad Wilson.

I also interviewed other external subject matter experts in state health care and government, including: Mike Darrow, former North Carolina Governors Jim Hunt and Jim Holshouser, Bill Pully, and Bob Seligson.

Others who provided invaluable research assistance and helped locate archival photos and materials were Eric Blevins, Laura Brown, Walt Campbell, Lois Cranford, Paul Cuadros, Robert Galbraith, Mike Keohane, Keith Longiotti, Amon Marstiller, Diana Mitchell, Jenifer Padilla,

John Schelp, Aidan Smith, Brigette Sullivan, Elizabeth Turner, Mira Waller, and Bradley Yelvington.

Jim Hutchison, Laura Kelly, and John Parker from the national Blue Cross Blue Shield Association generously assisted with securing photographic archives and manuscript review.

Documents, photos, and recollections about the design and construction of the iconic BCBSNC headquarters building were offered by Bruce Bland, Walter Bost, Rob Teer, and Gerald White.

The team in BCBSNC's Corporate Communications Department were my unflagging partners in developing both the strategic vision of this book and companion video, as well as managing its million details from beginning to end. I offer warm thanks to Heidi Deja, Cindy Gardiner, Lynne Garrison, Keith Hayes, Susan Lovett, and Patrick Sweeney for their persistence, good judgment, good humor, and excellent editorial eyes.

The considerable skills and patience of Chris Crochetière at BW&A Books brought this work to life in her elegant design and production of the book itself.

Finally, there are no words that can adequately express the thanks I owe my home team at Video Dialog Inc. for their hard work in support of this book and video: Dr. Steven Channing, Rebecca Cerese, Michael Davey, Warren Gentry, Cynthia Hill, John Klein, Jessye McDowell, Robert Newton, David Tyson, Judy VanWyk, and Tom Vickers.

To my partner, Barry Groner, you saw me through, as you always do.

Diana J. Newton

Introduction

The story of Blue Cross and Blue Shield of North Carolina (BCBSNC), the state's leading health insurer, is in many ways the story of North Carolina itself over the past 75 years. Since the company was founded in 1933, the state has undergone a remarkable transformation. From a population largely based on farms and small towns, dependent on an agricultural and basic manufacturing economy, North Carolina has grown to become one of the nation's largest states, driven by the success of the banking, health care, technical, and research industries that now thrive here. In parallel fashion, BCBSNC has experienced its own transformation—from selling hospital prepayment plans to employers in textile mills and tobacco factories to providing innovative health care products and cutting-edge health information via the Web to more than 3 million members. As the history of the state and the company are inextricably linked, so their futures will doubtless be joined.

This business history of Blue Cross and Blue Shield of North Carolina explores the complex intersections of politics and policy, of economics and social change, that have marked the course of the company's development. There has been a virtual revolution in the way that health care delivery and financing have developed from the era of the Great Depression to the dawn of the new millennium. It is evident in the distance from open-air surgery and bartering livestock for

Blue Cross and Blue Shield of North Carolina is one of the most valuable companies in our state. When you talk about a civic-minded company, they are it. They have a history of more than seventy years in our state, insuring more than three million of our people. Not only are they a great insurance company, which means people get good health care, but they go way beyond that. Blue Cross and Blue Shield of North Carolina has been a great partner of the state's leaders in constantly planning how to improve the health of all North Carolinians and joining with the state to provide the resources to do it.

—FORMER NORTH CAROLINA GOVERNOR
JAMES B. HUNT, JR.

medical care in the 1930s, to emergency transport by medical helicopter and computerized diagnostic procedures that are routinely used and commonly covered by health insurance today.

Yet it has been said that "history repeats itself." As the system has evolved, the tension between free-market and government-sponsored health care has been evident in the repeated cycles of legislation over the decades aimed at enacting national health insurance. All the while, the costs of health care have continually soared. While BCBSNC has demonstrated remarkable leadership in providing health care solutions for the citizens of North Carolina, it still faces complex problems rooted in deep paradoxes. While there are more people in North Carolina covered by health insurance than ever before, the percentage of people without coverage is also at its peak and above the national average. While information about good nutrition and fitness is widespread, an epidemic of obesity grows. As Blue Cross and Blue Shield of North Carolina grapples with such issues, perhaps a fresh look at its past will help inform the critical choices upon which the future health of North Carolina's people depends.

Chapter One

The Birth of the Blues in North Carolina

To understand how health care has evolved in North Carolina over the past 75 years, it is important to first examine the medical, socioeconomic, and political realities of the early twentieth century. These realities were harsh, as evidenced by the rapid spread of infectious diseases, high infant mortality rates, poor access to hospitals, and few dollars available to pay for doctor visits. The need for access to affordable health care was a problem in dire need of a solution—one that Blue Cross and Blue Shield of North Carolina would ultimately help provide for decades to come. The company's legacy of care began in the era of the Great Depression and has continued through the most revolutionary period of medical advances in history (see *Medical Developments through the Years*).

The State of Our State: The 1920s

It was a decade of polarities—prohibition and speakeasies, women's voting rights and the "Red Scare," creationism versus evolution in the Scopes Monkey Trial. A great migration of African Americans left the South for major cities and factory jobs in the North as Ku Klux Klan activity escalated. The national economy was shifting from agricultural to industrial. In 1920, and for the first time in U.S. history, more Americans were living in cities than on farms. This shift posed particular problems for the South. As President Franklin D. Roosevelt declared in his famous Four Freedoms speech, "The South presents right now the Nation's No. 1 economic problem."[1]

In North Carolina, the economy was still primarily agricultural, as it had been since colonial times. Over 80 percent of the state's population was rural—mostly

A tobacco farmer pauses for water. In 1920, 80 percent of North Carolina's population was rural, mostly struggling farm families with little access to health care and few dollars to pay for it when needed. Photo by Bayard Wootten, courtesy of the North Carolina Collection, University of North Carolina at Chapel Hill.

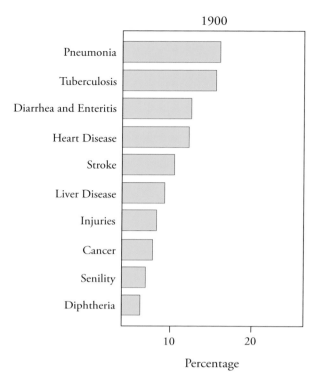

1900

Pneumonia	
Tuberculosis	
Diarrhea and Enteritis	
Heart Disease	
Stroke	
Liver Disease	
Injuries	
Cancer	
Senility	
Diphtheria	

10   20

Percentage

At the beginning of the 20th century, many diseases spread unchecked because of ineffective medical treatments, poor nutrition, contaminated water, and unsanitary living conditions. Graph courtesy of the National Center for Health Statistics.

farm families struggling to live off their crops and livestock. Tobacco was the big money crop, fueling the fortunes of a few, such as the Duke family of Durham, whose focus was on cigarette manufacturing. The demand for cotton had spawned the textile industry, where factory mill jobs had provided a more secure alternative to the uncertainty of working the land.

But the temporary boom created by a high demand for agricultural goods and textiles during the First World War had ended by the mid-1920s. In fact, North Carolina agriculture entered a depression two years before the legendary stock market crash of 1929. Apart from a handful of tobacco barons and textile magnates, most North Carolinians lived on the economic edge. Two-thirds of families earned $1,450 or less per year.

A severe public health crisis had also swept over the state during the war years, with thousands dying of typhoid fever and Spanish influenza. Half of North Carolina's 100 counties had no hospital. Likewise, there were few doctors, and poor country roads made reaching them even more difficult. The numbers in 1928 were dire: with only one doctor for every 1,244 people and one hospital bed for every 382 people, North

Carolina ranked 44th and 42nd, respectively, among the 48 states in the nation. To make matters worse, many people believed that they should go to the doctor or hospital only if they were near death. And with low family incomes, often near poverty level, it would prove nearly impossible for most to afford the ensuing medical bills brought on by an unexpected illness or accident. The severe financial hardship of hospitalization was compounded by the shame of being treated as a public "charity case." Some of those in need of treatment resorted to doing odd jobs such as painting at the hospital or offering chickens or meat in order to pay their bills.

Durham Visionaries Investigate the Idea of Hospital Prepayment

With mounting concern among community and government leaders about the lack of medical care, a visionary arrived in 1927 as the first dean of the newly formed Duke University School of Medicine. Dr. Wilburt C. Davison had heard about a hospital prepayment plan in use at the Roanoke Rapids Hospital for the employees of six area textile mills and their families. Mill families paid 25 cents per week under the Roanoke Rapids

Medical Developments Through the Years

Between 1900 and 1930, Americans suffered and died from diseases most of us can't even define today—pellagra and goiter, rickets and hookworm. During the 20th century, medical discoveries helped eliminate these and many other problems, and health insurance programs helped increasing numbers of average Americans pay for medical treatment.

Surgery in Avery County about 1920. In early 20th-century North Carolina, there were few hospitals and poor roads, so rural doctors were often forced to treat patients under primitive conditions. Photo by Bayard Wootten, courtesy of the North Carolina Collection, University of North Carolina at Chapel Hill.

Dr. W. C. Davison (above), first dean of the Duke University School of Medicine, and George Watts Hill (above, right), prominent Durham business leader. Together they founded the state's first hospital prepayment plan, the Hospital Care Association, in 1933. Photos courtesy of Duke University Medical Archives and the North Carolina Collection, University of North Carolina at Chapel Hill.

plan, which entitled them to ward beds in the community hospital. In addition, the mills employed several doctors and nurses, who provided free care to employees at home and in the hospital. Dr. Davison and Dr. Watson Rankin, director of the Duke Endowment, visited the city in 1927 to investigate how the plan worked and came away impressed: "We felt that if a prepaid medical and hospital program could work for mills in a single county, it might be successful for the state, and possibly for the nation."[2]

Enthusiastic about the prepayment idea, Dr. Davison set about trying to interest local business leaders and doctors in creating such a plan in Durham. He fully realized that the inability to pay hospital bills would undermine both individual health and the new Duke University Hospital's financial solvency. He found a receptive ear in George Watts Hill, board chairman of Durham's Watts Hospital. Watts Hospital had a proud heritage of being the first hospital in North Carolina to offer free care to those unable to pay. This generosity had kept the hospital dependent upon assistance from its founder, George Washington Watts, as the number of charity cases had reached a high of 47 percent in its early years of operation. George Watts Hill was committed to finding a solution to the problem of providing medical and surgical care to those who couldn't afford it. He began visiting local industrial leaders and eliciting their cooperation. With Hill's interest and influence, other Durham leaders shed their reservations and began offering support for the creation of a local hospital prepayment plan.

Dr. Davison also visited Oxford, England, where he had studied as a Rhodes scholar, to research what was known as the "Penny in the Pound" prepayment plan, created by the Radcliffe Infirmary and County Hospital. Integrating the best features of both the British and the Roanoke Rapids plans, as well as his own and Hill's ideas, Dr. Davison developed a new vision for a community-wide hospital prepayment plan. In August 1928, he wrote a paper entitled "The Hospital Association Plan as Applied to Durham." In it he announced the formation of a hospital association that would be affordable to the patient and could support the hospitals if even a minority of local citizens enrolled. A detailed description of Dr. Davison's plan was published in September 1928, including a schedule of benefits, proposed membership dues, and a method for collection.

A False Start on the Eve of the Depression

By the spring of the following year, both the vision and the support for a hospital prepayment plan were in place. On March 8, 1929, the Durham Hospital Association was organized at a meeting that members of the Chamber of Commerce, the Durham County Board of Health, the local Ministerial Association, and representatives from Watts, McPherson, and Lincoln Hospitals attended, pledging their cooperation and endorsement. The Association would not be operated for profit and would be open to any resident of Durham County, with a few exceptions based on health conditions. The group agreed that they would approach officials of the state's major industries, such as Erwin Mills and Liggett & Myers Tobacco Company, to gain support for promoting the plan to their employees.

Announcement of the Association's hospital prepayment plan appeared in the *Durham Morning Herald* on March 14, 1929, and described the basic dues and benefits. Over the next six months, membership applications and certificates were printed and equipment purchased in readiness for the Association's operational launch.

1920s

1929

In the late 1920s, half of North Carolina's 100 counties have no hospital. Only one doctor is available for every 1,244 people.

People from all over the country seek the "rest cure" for tuberculosis in the sanitaria of Asheville, N.C.

The Blue Cross Blue Shield Story

In 1929, mounting concern among Durham community and government leaders about the lack of medical care leads to the idea of a community-wide hospital prepayment plan.

Their vision is the beginning of a legacy of care and commitment to the people of North Carolina that would last into the next century.

But before the new Association had gotten off the ground, the economic bottom dropped out. On October 29, 1929—"Black Tuesday"—the stock market fell precipitously, signaling the start of the Great Depression. In the following years, 9,000 U.S. banks and 86,000 businesses failed. Wages plummeted by 60 percent and unemployment exceeded 25 percent, as the number of jobless rose to 15 million. Given this economic and social disaster, all activity toward establishing the Durham Hospital Association came to an abrupt halt. If the Depression had not disrupted Davison and Hill's progress, it would have been the first voluntary health service prepayment plan in the nation. But their passionate commitment to the idea remained, although their ability to relaunch the plan would have to lie dormant for several years until sufficient economic recovery had taken place.

As it turned out, a similar hospital prepayment plan was simultaneously founded in December 1929 by a prominent Dallas businessman, Justin Ford Kimball. For 50 cents per month, the city's schoolteachers paid in advance for hospital care through Baylor University. The Baylor Plan is known as the prototype upon which later Blue Cross Plans were based. In truth, the impetus to create hospital prepayment plans was taking root based on local initiative in diverse locations all over the nation. Doctors had become more supportive of the idea, as the Great Depression had led them to recognize the need for their patients to budget for their medical expenses in advance. Also, occupancy rates at voluntary hospitals nationwide were at record low numbers, and many went out of business. The time was ripe for a new approach. By the early 1930s, six plans that were similar in their service goals, yet rooted in local conditions, were operating in cities such as Cleveland, Newark, and Washington, D.C. These early hospital prepayment plans were founded as nonprofit organizations so that they didn't have to bear the overhead of taxes, which allowed a greater proportion of the membership fees to go directly toward payment of health care costs. Commercial health insurance carriers regarded the idea of prepayment as actuarially unsound, leaving the door open for voluntary public plans to gain ground with little competition.

1930

In 1930, the average life expectancy in the United States is 59.7 years. In North Carolina, it is even lower.

The federal government expands its role in public health protection and research by establishing the National Institutes of Health and the Food and Drug Administration in 1930.

Try, Try Again: The Hospital Care Association Is Born

Four years after the stock market crash, the idea for a local hospital prepayment association was revived in Raleigh by a group of businessmen led by Dwight Snyder. With encouragement from Rex and Mary Elizabeth Hospitals, they secured a charter on August 7, 1933, to organize a group hospitalization plan—the Hospital Care Association. A few days later, Snyder called upon George Watts Hill in Durham, who described his interest in prepayment efforts over the past five years and his continued interest in a statewide plan. Dr. Davison, too, became involved as one of the original board members. The new Hospital Care Association was the fourth Blue Cross Plan in the United States.

Although enthusiasm for the new organization was high among the six member hospitals in Raleigh and Durham, the benefits of a hospital prepayment plan had not been seeded in Raleigh as successfully as they had been in Durham during Davison and Hill's first attempt. It was a new concept that still seemed risky and untested to many. Snyder quickly approached Duke and Watts Hospitals for credit extensions of $1,000 each. A cash operating fund of only $250 was secured on a note signed by Hill, and a rent-free Durham office was set up in the downtown Trust Building. By November, E. M. Herndon, an original member of the Hospital Care

I Remember: "An idea was all he could offer . . . "

On September 22, 1933, Roy Medlin, formerly a printer in Raleigh, became the first subscriber ever enrolled by the Hospital Care Association. He remained continuously enrolled for more than 50 years. Medlin recalled: "A tall young man named Dwight Snyder entered my small print shop in downtown Raleigh with an idea. I soon discovered that an idea was all he could offer. We were all struggling to keep our businesses running without the use of cash, which in the year 1933 was very elusive.

"The idea seemed a very sound one to me and the trading began. Mr. Snyder wanted a used typewriter, application forms, and a few insurance policy forms to begin a new concept in the insurance field.

"After a few minutes of some deliberation, I knew he had me hooked, so I agreed to accept the first policy as payment for the items he needed to get him started."[3]

The first membership certificate issued by the Hospital Care Association in 1933 to Charles L. "Roy" Medlin. Photo courtesy of BCBSNC archives.

Well-baby clinic at Lincoln Hospital in Durham, 1938. In an effort to combat devastating maternal and infant mortality rates, hospitals began holding clinics to encourage hospital delivery and well-baby follow-up visits. Photo courtesy of Lincoln Hospital archives. Used with permission of Documenting the American South, the University of North Carolina at Chapel Hill Libraries.

Association founding group and later its first executive officer, was asked to move to the new Durham office in the role of sales manager.

With only one sales employee and a secretary, a desk and a phone, the Hospital Care Association began doing business. The first membership was bartered rather than sold. Roy Medlin, a Raleigh printer, and his wife agreed to become the first subscribers in exchange for printing the association's initial run of membership certificates (see *I Remember: "An idea was all he could offer . . ."*). At that time, coverage cost about two cents per day for an individual and seven cents per day for a family for 18 days of hospital care. Preexisting conditions such as pregnancy were covered, which set the stage for the birth of the nation's first "Blue Cross" baby, Ann Woodard, in December 1933. Her birth at Watts Hospital resulted in a $60 bill for 10 days to the Hospital Care Association. Early Plan administrators had been fearful of including maternity benefits for fear of an "epidemic" of babies, but Hospital Care's experience proved to be a desirable benefit for many. To others, though, "maternity care didn't mean a thing because most babies were born at home," as E. M. Herndon acknowledged

and the state's high maternal and infant mortality rates revealed.[4]

With the help of the two Durham hospitals' trustees and their employer friends, Herndon began a group membership drive. The *Durham Herald-Sun* newspaper became the first employee group of subscribers for the fledgling Association. The Duke University faculty was the next group to enroll. But what seemed like a sales coup actually precipitated a big financial loss for the new organization in its first year, as claims exceeded income from the Duke University group.

During 1934, Hospital Care gained membership traction, enrolling more than 4,000 members. That fall, Herndon traveled to the annual meeting of the American Hospital Association in Philadelphia to discuss the potential of prepayment with hospital administrators. It would prove to be the initial formal meeting of organizations that would later become the first Blue Cross Plans. Yet the financial losses continued, and Snyder became concerned about the Association's financial position. From the start, utilization rates had been greater than expected. Some board members thought that abuse by enrollees was to blame, while others thought that

In 1930, North Carolina's first four-year school of medicine and teaching hospital opens at Duke University.

In 1932, The U.S. Public Health Service begins the 40-year Tuskegee Syphilis Study on 600 African-American men in Alabama. In an infamous breach of ethics, study participants never receive the proper treatment for their illness.

In 1933–35, health insurance becomes available in North Carolina with the birth of the "Blue." The Hospital Care and Hospital Saving Associations are founded as rival "hospital prepayment plans," eventually merging to become Blue Cross and Blue Shield of North Carolina. For about $7 per year, an individual could cover himself for 18 days of hospital care. Family coverage costs about $25 per year.

An early membership certificate of the Hospital Saving Association, a rival hospital prepayment plan founded in 1935 and based in Chapel Hill. Like Hospital Care, it was one of the nonprofit parent organizations that would later become Blue Cross and Blue Shield of North Carolina. Photo courtesy of BCBSNC archives.

Membership Certificate

Issued By

HOSPITAL SAVING ASSOCIATION OF NORTH CAROLINA
(Incorporated)

Chapel Hill, N. C.

A Non-Profit Civic Organization

the Plan needed to shift toward a more qualitative selection of risks.

Ultimately, Snyder resigned, and the Hospital Care Association was reorganized. Duke and Watts Hospitals, still committed to the potential of the prepayment idea, provided an infusion of $6,000 each in capital to pay off the company's indebtedness. A new board was also elected to more closely direct the Plan's efforts to gain solid financial footing and credibility in the community. By the end of 1934, Hospital Care had opened its first district office in Asheville, and offices in Charlotte and Greensboro were added soon afterward.

Competition Close at Hand: The Hospital Saving Association

Many community leaders in the health care field had encouraged Hospital Care's formation. Among them was I. H. Manning, the former longtime dean of the University of North Carolina's School of Medicine and recent president of the North Carolina Medical Society. In a pattern remarkably similar to that of Hospital Care's founders, Manning, together with Graham Davis of the Duke Endowment, visited France and England in 1935 to study prepayment plans. They were convinced that the prepayment idea could meet the growing hospital care needs of North Carolina citizens and resolved to create a statewide, voluntary not-for-profit plan. With a $25,000 grant from the Duke Endowment, they filed a Charter of Incorporation for the Hospital Saving Association in March 1935.

The rival association opened its first office in Raleigh but quickly relocated to Chapel Hill's Public Health Building. The first certificates that Hospital Saving sold became effective on January 1, 1936. A group of schoolteachers in Charlotte was the first group enrolled by Hospital Saving. Fueled by its ambitious goal of enrolling 90 percent of the state's population, the new Plan grew quickly and by the end of 1936 had 14,395 members. Noting its rapid success, Hospital Care decided to extend its outreach beyond the confines of the Durham community. The business rivalry between the new Durham and Chapel Hill prepayment plans was under way. George Watts Hill admitted that "the folks in Durham" did not originally like the idea of competition but acknowledged that ultimately "competition keeps you smart. You don't get the chance to get lazy."[5]

Sales: The Old-Fashioned Way

Long before the advent of today's online applications and television advertising, the sales pitch was decidedly no-frills. As one of Hospital Saving's first salesmen, Bill Houck, recalled: "We spoke of enrolling people, we spoke of something you join, not something you bought. It was like a mutual aid society. Everybody would put their pennies in and help each other. It was a very simple concept. It was also simple in regard to the benefits and rates. Bed and board in a ward,

A snake-oil salesman approaches tobacco factory workers to pitch a questionable medical remedy. Fortunately, selling the new hospital prepayment idea in factories was met favorably—and provided a real health care value for workers and their families. Photo courtesy of the North Carolina Collection, Durham County Library.

I Remember: "Women put this thing on the map . . ."

Women sales representatives explain hospital prepayment options to Craven County turkey farmers. Photo courtesy of BCBSNC archives.

C. A. (Bill) Houck, Jr., began his 41-year career with Blue Cross and Blue Shield of North Carolina (BCBSNC) as a salesman for the Hospital Saving Association in 1938. Houck recalled: "When I went to work, as far as I know there was not a single man on the sales staff. They were all women. In the home office there were probably three or four men, and all the rest were women. Women really put this thing on the map. They believed in it, and they were terrific salespeople.

"Mrs. Stella Teague was the district manager for Hospital Savings in Winston-Salem. She was my boss, the one that hired me. She was operating her office under the staircase in her home in Old Salem. She was a terrific saleslady. She sold it like a religion. Within a year or two, she had 6,000 people enrolled. Subsequently, with the acquisition of Reynolds Tobacco Company and some other groups in about 1942, she had enrolled half the population of Winston-Salem! She gave me the best training I ever had.

"So I want to give a real accolade to the women because they were right up at the forefront of our early success."[9]

$3 a day credit toward a private room, which cost the whole of $5. We called it the '2 cents a day plan.'"[6] Although the commercial insurance carriers were largely skeptical about the potential profitability of hospital prepayment in those days, the general public seemed ready to accept the risk. Houck indicated that the idea appealed to both employers and employees alike. Initially, Hospital Saving sold exclusively to groups, while Hospital Care also sold to individuals.

The first step in the group sales effort was to gain buy-in to the prepayment plan from the employer. A group could be formed only if half or more of the employees enrolled, with a minimum requirement of ten people. Sometimes talking over the loud factory machines until he was hoarse, Houck often explained the prepayment concept to employees one by one.

If he was lucky, the employer might agree to shut down the factory machines for a short while so that he could make a group presentation and sign people up. The sales kit consisted of one simple folder that explained the entire Plan at a glance, an application card, and a receipt book in case he collected the membership dues up front. More often, the employer would deduct the dues from the employee's paycheck on behalf of the Plan.

But Hospital Saving sold to more than just major industrial employers. Payroll deductions for teachers were not authorized by the state, but teachers' membership dues were collected and transmitted by a group treasurer. The Plan also experimented with "pseudo groups"—a 75 percent employee enrollment rate could qualify several small businesses in one geographic area as a group. In rural areas, salespeople approached organizations such as the Grange, home demonstration clubs, and even rural churches.

Hospital Saving was, in fact, the only Plan in the nation with statewide operations, featuring members in 55 of North Carolina's 100 counties in its first two years (see *I Remember: "Women put this thing on the map . . ."*). Yet there was concern early on that its wider geographic scope, however altruistic in its intent, was proving to be more of a business burden than an advantage, as Hospital Care had better enrollment in 1936.[7] Both Plans' success was instead rooted in the support of local member hospitals, and those hospitals helped the young Associations gain access within the community. Interestingly, North Carolina was one of only two states with two Plans competing for business in the same market territory.[8]

Growth Strategies

Both health Plans had originated with the goal of improving access to hospital care for the working and lower classes, yet their early sales strategies posed something of a paradox. They began by targeting the professional and white-collar workers in order to "sell" the safety and viability of the prepayment idea. The strategy both worked and backfired. At first, the people who used the hospital the most were highly educated or working

I Remember: "When I hear an ambulance . . ."

Elisha M. Herndon helped found the Hospital Care Association in 1933 and became its first chief executive officer, serving for 35 years the organization that would later become Blue Cross and Blue Shield of North Carolina. Herndon recalled: "I can remember in those days seeing an ambulance headed for the hospital and saying, 'I hope the person in that ambulance isn't our member. We sure don't have the money to pay the claim.'

"Now when I hear an ambulance, I hope it is one of our members with our very best coverage because not only are we an organization that wants to render good service, we're now financially able to do so."[10]

Photo courtesy of BCBSNC archives.

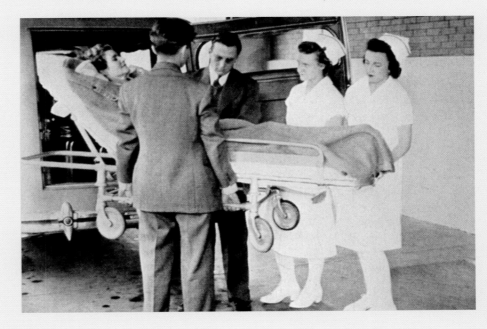

in health care, since they held less fear of doctors and hospitalization. Due to poor underwriting and higher-than-expected utilization rates, both Associations grew concerned about their financial losses. In fact, it took Hospital Care six years to realize its first slim operating profit (see *I Remember: "When I hear an ambulance . . ."*).

By late 1936, Hospital Care shifted its sales strategy toward those with lower incomes and began offering a less expensive certificate—two cents per day—identical to the rate schedule of Hospital Saving. Hospital Saving, too, had a primarily working- and lower-class membership base; 25 percent of its subscribers were textile workers, and 70 percent had incomes of less than $700 per year.[11] Many of its rural subscribers were aided by the health care provisions of the Farm Security Administration (FSA) program, established in 1937 to help farmers recover from the Great Depression. As a result, FSA became the first government program administered by the Hospital Saving Association.

There were particular challenges to successfully enrolling North Carolina's black citizens in the new prepayment plans. For example, of Durham's population of 60,000, one-third was African American, many of whom would qualify for low-cost hospitalization. But with the exception of tobacco factory employees, most of them worked in small industries, in retail stores, or for individuals and therefore could not be reached through group selling or collection by payroll deduction. As a result, sales representatives had to make individual calls and collect the dues personally. This proved to be an expensive practice: the membership cost for the same benefits of the original certificate was 50 percent greater for African Americans who were paid on a weekly basis. As E. M. Herndon acknowledged, "This increased cost to those least able to pay was a social and economic injustice."[12] In addition, in the racially segregated South of those days, concern about mixing white and black patients in the same hospital overwhelmed the need, and eventually the certificate was withdrawn.

The various sales strategies of the two Plans worked. By the late 1930s, Hospital Care's membership was doubling every year, and it had seven offices across the state. Although it had started operations two years later, Hospital Saving's growth quickly outstripped its competitor's membership numbers, exceeding 50,000 by 1937.

1933

Maternity benefits are included in hospital prepayment coverage, influencing more women to give birth in the safety and sanitary conditions of the hospital instead of at home, attended only by a midwife, general practitioner, or experienced relative.

The nation's first "Blue Cross baby," Ann Woodard, is born in December 1933, at Durham's Watts Hospital to parents enrolled in the new Hospital Care Association.

Earning Blue Cross Approval

As the prepayment movement grew, the annual meeting of the American Hospital Association (AHA) provided Plan leaders with an opportunity to share their local experiences and explore their challenges. By 1937, the AHA offered associate institutional membership to any nonprofit organization meeting its 14 standards, which were developed as a protective measure for both the public and the affiliated hospitals.[13] Approved Plans would qualify to display a symbol of affiliation—the Blue Cross. The AHA requested that both Hospital Care and Hospital Saving submit to an audit by an outside firm, with particular attention to their reserves. Both Associations subsequently agreed to institute the accounting plan suggested by the auditor. In addition, consideration was given to placing both Associations under the supervision of the North Carolina Department of Insurance, although they had originally been exempt from the state's insurance laws.[14]

On April 1, 1938, the Hospital Saving Association became one of the first 38 Plans approved to use the Blue Cross symbol. The Hospital Care Association gained approval later that year on September 1. The 40 organizations approved as "Blue Cross Plans" by the AHA in 1938 represented a total membership of almost 2 million people throughout the United States, clearly indicating that the nonprofit prepayment concept now had taken root on a national as well as a local basis, even though many Plans were still struggling financially.

Although Hospital Saving had won the honor of being the first association in North Carolina to qualify as a Blue Cross Plan, by 1939 it was approaching bankruptcy and in serious danger of losing Blue Cross approval. The new Plan needed decisive leadership at this critical moment, and found it in Eugene B. Crawford. Most of the fledgling plans stayed away from hiring people with insurance experience for management positions, because they thought the health and social welfare aspects of their missions were more relevant to their hiring philosophy.[15] Crawford had been a hospital administrator before coming to Hospital Saving, and his hospital knowledge and experience were pivotal in turning around the struggling Plan. He rapidly resolved the fiscal crisis by influencing its participating hospitals to accept 90 percent of the Plan's liability. Crawford was always committed to financial accountability, and under his leadership, Hospital Saving not only recovered but thrived, making remarkable gains in membership and introducing innovative programs.

Early Merger Discussions

In the wake of both Hospital Care and Hospital Saving gaining approval as Blue Cross Plans, the AHA began to exert some pressure for the two organizations to consolidate. In December 1938, the North Carolina Hospital Association

Hospital prepayment plans that met standards developed by the American Hospital Association to protect the public and hospitals were approved to display the Blue Cross symbol. Both N.C. Plans received Blue Cross approval in 1938. Photo courtesy of BCBSNC archives.

President Franklin D. Roosevelt signing the Social Security Act in 1935. While Social Security established important benefits for the elderly, it did not include health care. Voluntary rather than government-sponsored health insurance would provide access to affordable care for the rest of the century. Photo courtesy of the Library of Congress.

also came out in favor of the merger, listing the following advantages:

1. The merged membership would be as strong or stronger financially.
2. A strong and smooth-running organization would serve to ward off state government-sponsored medicine.
3. The unpleasant and antagonistic rivalry would be abolished.
4. Operating expenses could be decreased.
5. Group claims could be reduced.
6. Political pressure by individuals could be diminished.
7. More satisfaction of contracts could be achieved by utilization of the experiences of both organizations.[16]

Certainly these were undeniably sound business reasons, and a committee comprising representatives of both Hospital Care and Hospital Saving was established to study the feasibility of a merger. But negotiations floundered over issues of board structure and Plan identity, indicating a lack of willingness to genuinely overcome the Plans' differences. Whatever the root cause of the failure to reach agreement, this consolidation effort would prove to be the first of many that would ultimately continue for another 30 years before coming to fruition.

Medicine and Government Take Notice

The Social Security Act had passed in 1935, providing a range of benefits for the elderly, but it did not include provisions for health care. With prepayment plans gaining acceptance throughout the country, the federal government began to explore the idea of compulsory national health insurance. As early as 1938, the Roosevelt administration organized a conference on the topic of national health programs and included "consideration of a general medical care program supported by taxes, insurance, or both."[17] In 1939, Senator Robert F. Wagner introduced the first "National Health Bill" (S. 1620), which incorporated the recommendations that had emerged from the National Health Conference held in Washington, D.C., a few months earlier to address problems in medical care. The bill proposed a national compulsory health insurance for almost all employees and their dependents, with benefits to include physicians' services, hospitalization, drugs, and laboratory diagnostic services. Costs would be covered through employer and employee contributions deposited in a health insurance fund. The plan was to be administered through the states.

Although the bill died in committee, the forces of organized medicine took serious note and began to back private hospitalization insurance in a more pronounced way. With the growing popularity of hospital prepayment, there had been increasing public demand for the development of similar service plans that would cover the provision of medical services, not just surgical care and hospitalization. The medical establishment recognized this demand as a realistic threat that could open the door to government-controlled medical care and diminish the quality of patient care as well as an opportunity to retain control of the provision of medical services by the doctors themselves. As a result, the American Medical Association (AMA) formally endorsed voluntary hospitalization insurance but with an important caveat—"providing all such plans do not incorporate medical service or medical care."[18] Instead, the AMA advocated for state and local medical societies to address their community's needs by forming medical plans of their own.

1935

A crown jewel of FDR's New Deal, the Social Security Act, passes. In failing to provide for health care coverage, it solidifies an American paradigm: that health coverage in the United States would be funded largely by individuals or employers, not the government.

1936

By 1936, Hospital Saving has members in 55 of 100 North Carolina counties.

In 1936, a Duke physician originates the use of ultraviolet radiation to control airborne infections in surgical operating rooms, a technique that has become widely accepted across the country.

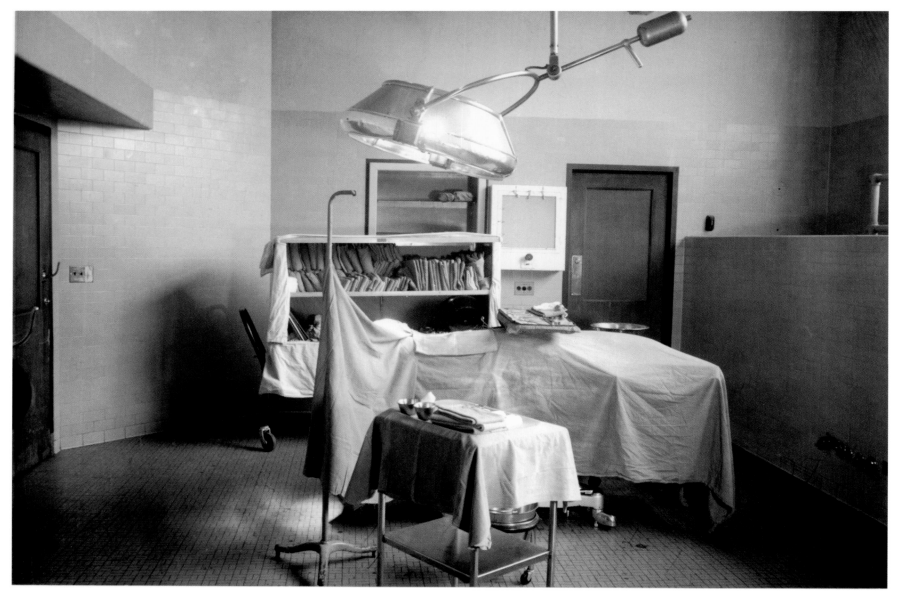

An operating room prepared for surgery with ultraviolet light, X-ray screen, instrument table, and patient bed. The use of ultraviolet radiation to control airborne infections was an innovative surgical practice in 1936. Photo courtesy of Duke University Medical Center Archives.

Hospital Care Association's 1933 charter had included provisions for the sale of surgical care, but as of the late 1930s, the Plan had not yet enacted such coverage and wanted the physicians themselves to provide the underwriting for any medical benefits. Hospital Saving Association also wanted to add surgical benefits to its coverage, but its original charter did not provide for them. The North Carolina Medical Society had been a committed sponsor of Hospital Saving since its inception, actively influencing the direction and management of its operations. Leaders within the Medical Society recognized the need to expand into the medical market but wanted to proceed cautiously.

In the meantime, the commercial carriers resumed their interest in providing health insurance. Although they had considered "sickness insurance" too risky during the formative years of the prepayment movement, by the late 1930s they recognized a growing market and became an additional source of competition for both of North Carolina's nonprofit Plans. They began offering contracts with a limited schedule of surgical benefits, which became particularly popular with the state's key industries, especially textiles.

The 1930s had seen North Carolina's fledgling hospital prepayment plan, the Hospital Care Association, derailed by the depths of the Great Depression, then reborn out of the vision of a few pioneers who started with only a handful of dollars but with a determination to serve the profound health care needs in the state. The Hospital Care Association found a growing market in the state—and, with it, competition from the nearby Hospital Saving Association. In less than a decade, these two Plans had provided more than 100,000 North Carolinians with better access to health care. The roots of Blue Cross and Blue Shield of North Carolina were taking hold.

1937

In 1937, the infant death rate for babies under one year of age in Durham County, N.C., is 52.2 per 1,000 live births among whites and 94.2 per 1,000 among African Americans. Clinics are held weekly at Lincoln Hospital to encourage hospital delivery and well-baby follow-up visits.

1938

In 1938, the Hospital Saving Association becomes one of the first Plans approved by the American Hospital Association to use the Blue Cross symbol. Hospital prepayment plans are taking root across the country.

1939

In 1939, research demonstrates penicillin's ability to kill infectious bacteria.

Chapter Two

A Campaign for Good Health in North Carolina

Medical and Surgical Coverage Offered

By the eve of the Second World War, the growing popularity of hospital prepayment plans had demonstrated that this was indeed the wave of the future. Physicians across the nation recognized that they needed to respond to this growing demand in creative new ways. If people wanted coverage for hospitalization, why not encourage better medical and surgical care through prepayment plans as well? Commercial health insurance carriers had begun to success-fully compete by doing so. In North Carolina, the Hospital Care and Hospital Saving Associa-tions continued to consider how they could offer additional benefits so that more of the state's citizens could have improved access to affordable health care.

In 1940, when the lucrative contract for Erwin Cotton Mills came up for bid, Hospital Care recognized a critical opportunity to fulfill its social mission and offer health protection to the workers and their families. Erwin Mills, the state's first manufacturer of denim, had a large—and vulnerable—workforce for its time. The 5,000 employees working the looms in the company's six mill buildings were at significant risks for musculoskeletal injuries, auditory damage from excessive machinery noise, and unregulated amounts of textile dust, which could result in respiratory illnesses such as "brown lung." While hospital coverage would help, they could certainly benefit from better access to physicians and surgeons too.

Hospital Care quickly organized the Medical Service Association as a separate corporation, primarily to enroll the employees of Erwin Mills. Though some of the Medical Service Association directors also served on the board of Hospital Care, the new organization had a separate financial structure, accounting, and reserves, and it was underwritten by physicians in the county

Textile workers in mills across North Carolina were vulnerable to machinery accidents and illnesses such as brown lung. Photo courtesy of the Southern Historical Collection, Wilson Library, the University of North Carolina at Chapel Hill.

medical societies surrounding the various mill locations. The Medical Service Association began by offering minimal surgical and in-hospital medical benefits, charging a mere $2 fee for a hospital visit. The maximum benefit for physician care was $100 per year, which was intended to provide only partial coverage for subscribers. It was, nevertheless, a precursor to what would soon become Blue Shield coverage.

Not to be outdone by its primary competitor, Hospital Saving also began offering a surgical benefits program in 1940. But unlike Hospital Care, its charter did not allow for the sale of surgical care, and the insurance commissioner pointed out the illegality of the new program. One of Hospital Savings' founders, Dr. I. H. Manning, then approached the North Carolina Medical Society for permission to add medical and surgical benefits, and his request was approved. The next step would be at the legislative level.

Both Plans had originally been exempt from North Carolina's insurance laws. But they had agreed, under some pressure from the American Hospital Association at the time of their Blue Cross approvals in 1938, to work toward securing regulatory oversight of nonprofit organizations

of their type. In 1941, the state legislature passed a bill (S.B. 128)—now Chapter 57 of the General Statutes—that established regulation of nonprofit hospital service organizations by the State Commissioner of Insurance. The key provisions required the Plans to submit rates and contracts for approval, to establish reserves for contingencies, and to limit the size and type of investments.[1] Both Plans regarded the legislation favorably, as they believed it imbued their operations with even greater credibility and a sense of financial security that would increase the public trust. With the passage of this bill and changes made to its enabling act, the Hospital Saving Association could now sell its program of surgical benefits legally and resume competition for this new market.

Blue Shield Emerges amid Physician Resistance

As with the grassroots development of Blue Cross Plans throughout the 1930s, medical prepayment plans such as the Medical Service Association were springing up in communities across the nation by the end of the 1940s. The Blue Shield concept—prepayment plans for

In 1940, the average life expectancy in the United States is 62.9 years. In North Carolina, it remains even lower.

More than 22,000 new cases of syphilis and other venereal diseases are reported in North Carolina, posing a major concern for the many young draftees coming to Fort Bragg.

North Carolina's Blue Plans first offer surgical insurance and come under the regulatory oversight of the State Insurance Commissioner in 1941.

medical services—had grown out of the lumber and mining camps of the Pacific Northwest, where serious injuries and chronic illnesses were common among workers in these hazardous jobs. Similar conditions in North Carolina's textile mills and tobacco manufacturing plants gave rise to the same desire on the part of employers to provide medical care for their workers through contracted physician services.

Physician resistance to such plans was initially and consistently high based on their pervasive concerns about control of their fees for medical services. Traditionally, doctors had been free to set their own fees, usually on an "each according to his ability to pay" basis. They would accept some patients they knew would never pay, while charging wealthier patients higher fees in order to compensate. But medical service prepayment plans did offer some distinct advantages. First, they were relieved of having to make the determination about who could pay and no longer had to risk nonpayment. The plans also increased the ability of lower-income patients to pay, which ultimately benefited the doctors.

As in North Carolina, enabling legislation allowing the establishment of medical service organizations had passed in a half dozen other states by the early 1940s. Yet many state medical societies attempted to maintain some degree of physician control by exerting pressure in favor of limited coverage, voluntary physician participation, and free choice of providers for subscribers. Others saw the choice differently: either

Erwin Mills, the state's largest manufacturer of denim, first offered surgical and medical benefits to its employees in 1940. Letter courtesy of BCBSNC archives.

THE ERWIN COTTON MILLS COMPANY

K.P. Lewis, President & Treasurer
John Sprunt Hill, 1st Vice-President
J.C. Thorne, 2nd Vice-President
W.H. Ruffin, Secretary & Asst Treasurer

West Durham Station
Durham, N. C.

No. 1 Mill Durham, N.C.
" 2 " Erwin, N.C.
" 3 " Cooleemee, N.C.
" 4 " Durham, N.C.
" 5 " Erwin, N.C.
" 6 " Durham, N.C.

June 28, 1940

TO OUR EMPLOYEES:

For the past three years a great proportion of our employees have been members of The Hospital Care Association, and our information is that this plan has worked well and satisfactorily. There have been a good many requests made to add surgical and medical benefits.

Through full cooperation of the Durham and Orange County Medical Society, a new non-stock, and non-profit association has been formed which offers these benefits. We have studied several plans, and believe that this plan, which has the cooperation of your local medical society, offers more service for the dues charged than any other plan.

We are allowing representatives to present the plan to you, and suggest that you give it your full consideration. We believe it is a good plan. We have no financial interest whatever in either The Hospital Care Association, or the newly formed Medical Service Association, but we will be glad, if you desire to join them, to make the weekly deduction of dues at your request.

Faithfully yours,

THE ERWIN COTTON MILLS COMPANY

By: _____
President and Treasurer

KPL.Y

participate in voluntary medical prepayment plans or face the prospect of compulsory health insurance administered by the state.[2]

With the advent of medical prepayment plans, other conflicts began brewing as well. Hospital-based specialists, such as anesthesiologists, pathologists, and radiologists, bristled at having their fees included in the hospital benefit schedule but also balked at attempts to regulate their charges within medical prepayment programs. Subscribers were often surprised and unhappy to receive a separate bill from such specialists in addition to their regular hospital bill. There were also complexities in the relationship between the Blue Cross Plans, which offered hospital prepayment, and the newer Blue Shield Plans, which offered coverage for medical services. Hospital Care maintained a separate corporate structure and board from its Medical Service Association, but the two shared an office, equipment, and administrative staff on an as-needed basis, which sometimes resulted in confusion. For all these reasons, tension infused both the concept and implementation of medical prepayment programs.

Wartime Politics and the Impact on Health Care

Following Pearl Harbor and the entry of the United States into World War II in December 1941, the health care market changed dramatically. President Franklin Roosevelt announced ambitious wartime production goals. Unemployment dropped to 1.2 percent. As a result, all of the country's economic sectors came under new or increased government controls. For example, the creation of the National War Labor Board in 1942 resulted in wage restrictions. Employers who needed to attract labor were compelled to resort to offering a growing range of fringe benefits, including better pensions, medical insurance, and paid holidays and vacations. Health insurance may well have been the most popular of these benefits, and employer contributions became the norm that continues today. There were also federal income tax incentives for group insurance, which quickly began to overtake individual policies as the most popular form of coverage.

The idea of compulsory health insurance was, in fact, gaining momentum in the early 1940s. Although the 1939 National Health Act Bill had failed to pass, President Roosevelt recommended

1942

In 1942, President Franklin D. Roosevelt recommends compulsory national health insurance in his State of the Union address, but Congress blocks his effort to establish it.

1943

The antibiotic streptomycin is discovered in 1943. By the end of the 1940s it will virtually eradicate tuberculosis in the United States.

During World War II, North Carolina leads the nation in the rate of rejection of its draftees for medical reasons.

1944

The use of penicillin and sulfa drugs during World War II significantly reduces the number of deaths and amputations caused by infected wounds among Allied forces, saving an estimated 12–15 percent of lives.

compulsory health insurance in his 1942 State of the Union address. But support for his war efforts was not matched by equivalent support for his programs on the domestic front. Congress dismantled New Deal agencies such as the Works Progress Administration and blocked his effort to establish national health insurance. In 1943, the first of what would be three versions of the Wagner-Murray-Dingell bill sought to add national health insurance to the Social Security system but never came to a vote in Congress. Though many organized labor and farm organizations had supported the bill, it was vigorously opposed by representatives of organized physicians, who regarded it as "socialized medicine" that could endanger patients, limit their choice of physicians, and regulate medical practice and income. In his 1945 State of the Union address, Roosevelt outlined an "Economic Bill of Rights" that included "the right to adequate medical care and the opportunity to achieve and enjoy good health," but no specific proposal for health insurance was made in the wake of his passionate appeal. For the time being, the possibility of government-sponsored health insurance was tabled.

Nonetheless, Roosevelt's belief that many Americans needed better health care was certainly accurate. Prior to the end of the war, 42 percent of U.S. counties had no community hospital, and many of those in existence were substandard. In North Carolina, statistics from our potential draftees told a disturbing story:

The production of penicillin significantly reduced the number of deaths and amputations among Allied forces during World War II. Photo courtesy of Schenley Laboratories.

Poor health among North Carolinians in the early 1940s was evident in the rejection rates of World War II inductees, high infant mortality, and rampant childhood diseases. Photo courtesy of the Southern Historical Collection, Wilson Library, the University of North Carolina at Chapel Hill.

41 percent of whites and 61 percent of blacks had been rejected because of health reasons. When compared to young men of the same age and both races who had been raised in North Carolina orphanages, the rejection rate for health reasons was less than 2 percent. The national rate of rejection stood at 30 percent. Only different levels of access to health care could explain this staggering discrepancy.[3]

Beginning in 1942, the war effort included nationwide rationing of many commodities. Foods such as sugar, butter, coffee, and beef were scarce. Many Americans began to cultivate "Victory Gardens" of fresh vegetables to supplement their sometimes sparse diets and as a show of patriotism. In addition, the consumption of clothing, shoes, coffee, gasoline, tires, and fuel oil was also rationed. As a young salesman for the Hospital Saving Association, Bill Houck described the uncertainties of business travel during the war years: "I traveled by car until my ration of gas gave out and then traveled by bus or train. We had no one to supervise our business in the eastern half of the state, and I found myself going down there by bus or hitching a ride with someone who had some gas left" (see *I Remember: A beat-up Chevrolet. . .*).[4]

As World War II progressed, hospitalization rates increased dramatically, with admissions to nonprofit hospitals doubling in the decade from 1935 to 1946. With that increase, there was also a scarcity of hospital beds and an upward spiral in costs. The implications for North Carolina's young prepayment plans were similarly dramatic and yet paradoxical. Although Hospital Care's membership grew at the fastest rate in its history, adding 50,000 new subscribers during the war years, its reserves were also dropping at a worrisome rate of 2.5 percent each year over the same period. Plan leaders thought they could not safely raise rates without affecting the lapse ratio (the number of memberships that have lapsed within a specified period of time compared to those in force at the beginning of the period), which they deemed too high. As Hospital Care's Board President B. R. Roberts lamented, "We are dying of improvement year by year."[6]

North Carolinians had begun to warm to the idea of hospital and medical prepayment, but overall they were still not consistently accessing and receiving adequate health care. By the end of World War II, the 1946 rankings revealed that North Carolina had made little progress in improving the health status of its citizens in the years since the Great Depression. Tuberculosis was still proving an insidious disease; almost 1,200 North Carolinians died of it in 1945. The tuberculosis mortality rate for African Americans was 66.6 percent, more than three times higher than that for whites. In an effort to support those suffering with it, the Hospital Care Association had begun paying tuberculosis claims at recognized hospitals in 1944. But the numbers remained dire until a powerful antibiotic was developed to combat tuberculosis. North Carolina was, in fact, suffering in many ways. Although

I Remember: "A beat-up Chevrolet . . ."

J. Gray McAllister, Jr., began his long career with Blue Cross and Blue Shield of North Carolina as the director of Research and Statistics for the Hospital Saving Association in 1945. McAllister recalled: "During the war, the Association had one automobile—a beat-up Chevrolet of relatively ancient vintage. Bill Houck and I went with Mr. Eugene B. Crawford and several others in this jalopy on a trip to Cincinnati. We stopped overnight in Bluefield, West Virginia, where an attendant noticed a bulge on the tire the size of a cantaloupe. The spare tire was completely unsafe, and there was a real question as to

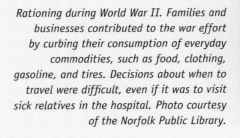

Rationing during World War II. Families and businesses contributed to the war effort by curbing their consumption of everyday commodities, such as food, clothing, gasoline, and tires. Decisions about when to travel were difficult, even if it was to visit sick relatives in the hospital. Photo courtesy of the Norfolk Public Library.

whether we were going to spend the rest of the war years in Bluefield, when the attendant asked us if we would like to have some new tires. This was during the time when new tires were unattainable for other than the military. But Mr. Crawford went along with the joke, stating that he would like to have two new tires. The attendant went down the street and returned in a few minutes with a new tire over each shoulder, which were sold to us at pre-war prices. Though others in Bluefield undoubtedly did know, these particular people apparently either did not know or did not care that the war was going on. They even refused to take our gas ration tickets, saying they had no use for them."[5]

Enrollment in N.C. Blue Plans grew at record rates during the war years, but the state needed more hospitals to keep up with the health care needs of its citizens. Photo courtesy of the BCBSNC archives.

the state was the 11th most populous (in 1940), it placed 42nd in number of available hospital beds, 45th in physicians, 37th in infant mortality, 44th in per capita income, and 46th in literacy.

These health statistics hardly prepared the state's citizens to ward off the rising national incidence of polio—also known as infantile paralysis—nationwide. The disease was known for brutally paralyzing children in particular, resulting in, at best, their confinement to wheelchairs and crutches and, at worst, treatment in a respiratory device known as the "iron lung." North Carolina was hit hard by a series of polio epidemics between 1944 and 1954. The most devastating of these wracked the town of Hickory in Catawba County in 1944. With the support of the National Foundation for Infantile Paralysis, a local camp was quickly converted into an emergency hospital, admitting 450 mostly young patients within a few months. Thanks to the local and national resources that were mobilized, the outbreak was brought under control, and the hospital closed by 1945.[7]

Given these kinds of health crises, both federal and state policymakers recognized the need for a concerted, government-sponsored effort to improve health outcomes by fighting

1945

From 1938 to 1948, a major shift from home to hospital deliveries is occurring throughout the country, a result of encouragement by medical professionals and affordable costs for families having hospital insurance. During this time, the proportion of infants born in hospitals increases from 55 percent to 90 percent.

While hospital births are more prevalent than midwife-assisted births among white, middle- to upper-class women, the tradition of midwife-assisted births continues in rural areas, particularly among African Americans.

In 1945, the N.C. State Board of Health initiates the first program related to the prevention and cure of cancer.

deadly diseases and improving the health care infrastructure. To address the latter, the Hospital Survey and Construction Act, co-sponsored by Senators Harold Burton and Lister Hill, was enacted by Congress in 1946. Widely known as the Hill-Burton Act, it originally provided federal grants to build and modernize hospitals in underserved areas identified by the states. Since 33 of its counties had no hospital, North Carolina became eligible for $17 million over a five-year period for construction of public and nonprofit hospitals and community health care centers, especially in rural areas. To obtain those funds, each dollar had to be matched by two dollars of state, county, or local money.

The Good Health Campaign Brings Stars, Slogans, and Statistics to North Carolina

At the same time that the Hill-Burton legislation was being enacted in Congress, North Carolina Governor J. Melville Broughton decided to create a commission specifically to address the state's persistent health care problems. In 1944, he appointed the State Hospital and Medical Care Commission to study health conditions and develop a program of improvement. Led by Dr. Clarence Poe, editor of the *Progressive Farmer* magazine, and 50 other leaders from diverse professions, the Poe Commission focused on three pressing needs: more doctors, more hospitals, and more nonprofit health service insurance. After a year of study, the Poe Commission made

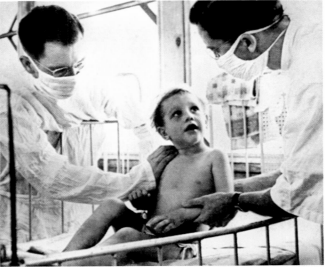

*"In the town of Hickory, in the western foothills of North Carolina, more than 100 children lie in hastily built beds. . . . The suddenness with which the disease struck overwhelmed ordinary medical facilities. . . . The National Foundation for Infantile Paralysis mobilized local and national resources to set up the emergency hospital" (*LIFE *magazine, 1944). Photos courtesy of Marc Shell.*

The federal Hill-Burton Act of 1946 and the state Good Health Plan provided funding to build badly needed hospitals in underserved areas of North Carolina. Photo courtesy of the Southern Historical Collection, Wilson Library, the University of North Carolina at Chapel Hill.

its report to the 1945 legislature, issuing the following recommendations:

1. Develop a state-supported four-year medical school.
2. Provide loan funds for medical students.
3. Provide medical training for black youths.
4. Appropriate $5 million to assist counties and communities in building and enlarging hospitals.
5. Provide state encouragement for the development of group medical care plans.[8]

In 1945, the legislature passed a bill making the N.C. Medical Care Commission a permanent state agency and endorsing its recommendations, which had been expanded into a six-point "Good Health Plan" that added funding for hospitalization of indigent patients to the recommendations of the Poe Commission.

The state Medical Care Commission's campaign to improve health conditions quickly went into high gear. It formed the N.C. Good Health Association (NCGHA) as a public relations agency charged with building public awareness of the Commission's programs. Dr. I. G. Greer, a well-respected college history professor, accepted the role of president, and H. C. Cranford, who would later serve as vice president of public relations for Blue Cross and Blue Shield of North Carolina, became the executive director of the Good Health Association. When Kay Kyser, a famous orchestra leader, radio and movie star of that era, and Rocky Mount native, visited his home state for vacation in 1946, he met with Dr. Greer and learned about the goals of the Good Health Association. Kyser was roused to action and suggested that the Association "start a bonfire at the grassroots" by using all known methods of publicity to build a greater awareness of the state's health status among North Carolinians. He stopped his vacation and visited 30 of the state's 100 counties, giving speeches and raising funds for the Good Health campaign and serving as its honorary vice president. Kyser's star power brought unprecedented visibility to the comprehensive multimedia campaign that he and Cranford devised, which would unrelentingly promote the core slogan—"North Carolina's No. 1 Need . . . Good Health!"—over the next year.

The Good Health publicity kickoff began at 7 p.m. on November 9, 1946, with a live radio broadcast featuring a host of screen and radio stars, particularly those from North Carolina. Led by Kay Kyser, Hollywood luminaries of the day such as Ava Gardner (of Johnston County), Kathryn Grayson (of Winston-Salem), Randolph Scott (of Charlotte), Red Skelton, and Dinah Shore performed skits, sang songs, and shared

facts and stories that highlighted the state's health care needs. The 30-minute program was broadcast over every one of the state's 47 full-time radio stations and heard by over a million people. The next day was promoted as "Good Health Sunday," and ministers were encouraged to use the occasion to deliver "health sermons" to their congregations.

Over the following months, the Good Health campaign in North Carolina used a wide variety of approaches to improve North Carolinians' awareness of the state's dire public health status. Additional star-driven 30-minute radio shows were broadcast on Thanksgiving, Christmas, and New Year's Day, 1947. Kyser convinced performers such as popular jazz singer and composer Hoagy Carmichael, the legendary comedy team of George Burns and Gracie Allen, and radio program characters Fibber McGee and Molly to participate in regular 15-minute shows airing across North Carolina.

Kyser was also certain that many people would never read about the state's bad health record or listen to a speaker share the startling statistics. But he thought they might be reached through a musical appeal. He asked famed lyricist Sammy Cahn and composer Jule Styne to write a song

North Carolina's 1945 health report card is dismal: 33 of 100 counties have no hospital; 39 counties have no hospital beds for African Americans; the state ranks 45th in the number of physicians, 37th in infant mortality, and 40th in maternal mortality.

Congress enacts the Hill-Burton Act in 1946, providing federal grants to build and modernize hospitals in underserved areas. North Carolina receives $17 million in matching funds over a five-year period.

In 1946, North Carolina launches the Good Health Program, a comprehensive plan to improve state health conditions through public awareness, educating and recruiting more doctors, building more hospitals, and developing more group medical care through nonprofit insurers such as the Blue Plans.

Under the leadership of orchestra leader Kay Kyser (top), many high-profile entertainers offered their talents to publicize the Good Health Campaign in North Carolina. Such star power included screen actress Ava Gardner (left), comedian Red Skelton (right), and a recording by Frank Sinatra and Dinah Shore (bottom). Photos courtesy of the Southern Historical Collection, Wilson Library, the University of North Carolina at Chapel Hill.

to help with the cause. Within 24 hours, they delivered "It's All Up to You (to Make North Carolina No. 1 in Good Health)," which was then donated to North Carolina's Good Health campaign. In their only performance together, Frank Sinatra and Dinah Shore recorded the song, and Columbia Records donated 10,000 copies to the NCGHA for promotional give-aways. "It's All Up to You" first aired in January 1947, and local radio stations decided how to give away their share of the free copies to enthusiastic listeners.

In addition to the radio promotion of good health, a series of movie trailers played in theaters, and 16-millimeter health films were produced and distributed to schools, agencies, and public institutions. Many North Carolina newspapers published weekly health features, and the NCGHA issued daily press releases. Talks by state leaders and prominent citizens such as Governor R. Gregg Cherry and George Watts Hill drew large audiences to hear facts about the state's poor health status. Hill's speeches appealed not only to the humanitarian benefits of the Good Health Plan but also to business interests. He pointed out that the program could result in enormous savings to labor and industry by

cutting down the state's rate of worker absentee-ism due to illness, which was higher than the national average.

The campaign also posted a series of roadside billboards with dramatic scenes in which messages such as "Get a Doctor!" and "Where's the Hospital?" communicated the state's need for more physicians and health care facilities. Window displays, lapel buttons, postage meter ads, even milk bottle collars proclaimed the Good Health campaign slogans. Famous cartoonists contributed comic strips to newspapers in order to help.

In schools across the state, dramatic skits were performed and an oratorical contest was held among high school students to determine who could deliver the most compelling 10-minute speech about why good health should matter to all North Carolinians. Finalists proceeded from local to regional and state levels of competition as their talks were recorded and aired in their local communities. There were, however, separate contests for white and black students—a sign of the still-segregated times in our state. The grand prize was a $500 college scholarship to the winning boy and girl orator in each division. There was also a competition for the title of "Miss

1946

The Hospital Saving Association contracts with the Veterans Administration in 1946 to cover home treatment for returning N.C. veterans with service-related disabilities.

The prospect of national health insurance reemerges in 1946 under President Harry Truman but is again defeated.

1947

In the postwar recovery period, unionized labor gains a strong negotiating position for health benefits with the passage of the Taft-Hartley Act in 1947.

North Carolina is battered by a series of polio epidemics from 1944 to 1954. Sadly, the state leads the nation in polio cases reported in 1948.

1948

In response to the epidemics, N.C. Blue Plans offer additional coverage for polio and other "dread diseases." For only $5 per year, a family could receive benefits up to $6,000 for medical and hospital bills, as well as the braces, crutches, and wheelchairs polio sufferers often needed.

North Carolina Student Nurse," who was ultimately crowned by Kay Kyser himself in a manner reminiscent of the Miss America pageant.

The week of February 2–8, 1947, was proclaimed Good Health Week in the public schools as a means of improving health instruction, health examinations, and physical education. In a speech the following week, Governor Cherry urged North Carolinians to give "serious" consideration to joining Blue Cross for hospitalization insurance. "In recognition of the humanitarian achievements of the Blue Cross Plan of this state," Cherry declared, "I wish to call attention to the week of February 18 to 23 as Blue Cross Week." The governor acknowledged that Blue Cross service had become "a vital part of the life and health of the entire state."[9]

The intensive Good Health campaign concluded in March 1947 after an unparalleled effort to raise the awareness of North Carolina citizens about their health problems and the solutions outlined in the Good Health Plan. Both the recommendations of the Poe Commission and the public health awareness created by the Good Health campaign ultimately provided even more growth opportunities for Hospital Care and Hospital Saving in the postwar economy. The two Associations conducted successful community enrollment drives statewide to help meet the goals of more nonprofit health insurance identified by the Good Health Plan. These drives particularly targeted farm families who badly needed affordable hospital coverage, resulting in

Hospital Saving's enrollment of both the North Carolina Grange and North Carolina Farm Bureau Federation in 1947.

Over the next five years, the implementation of the Good Health Plan would cost a total of $48 million, one-third of which would be paid by the federal government from the Hill-Burton program and the remaining two-thirds by matching funds from state and local governments. The majority of these dollars were allocated for the addition of 7,200 hospital beds, while half a million dollars was earmarked to provide one dollar a day for patients who could not pay for their hospital care. Although North Carolina citizens certainly benefited from the additional beds, there was a shadow side to this increase in hospital infrastructure: the debt service on the matching funds required under the Hill-Burton grant program was a significant new expenditure. Along with the rising rates of room, board and nursing care, technological advances, new medicines, and a general rebound from wartime price and wage controls, this higher debt service contributed to a steep increase in costs to hospitals—and to the hospital prepayment plans.

Postwar Developments

With the death of Franklin Roosevelt, Harry Truman became president and navigated the nation through the transition from war to peacetime. Wage and cost controls were lifted, and Blue Cross and Blue Shield Plans across the nation were beginning to struggle with the rapidly escalating costs of hospitalization and health care delivery in general. The prospect of national health insurance reemerged in 1946, when a revised version of the Wagner-Murray-Dingell bill was reintroduced to Congress and embraced by Truman. The AMA, now entrenched in opposition to the bill, waged an extensive campaign to defeat the legislation. The 1947 resolutions adopted by the N.C. Medical Society acknowledged the perceived threat, describing it as "national propaganda for compulsory health insurance."[10] The front-page debate over health insurance policy prompted by the Wagner-Murray-Dingell legislation marked another bout in the recurrent fight over national health care reform policy.

Throughout the war years, Hospital Care and Hospital Saving had continued to offer their new surgical and medical prepayment services. As of 1943, Hospital Care had begun writing surgical benefits into its own coverage rather than that of the Medical Service Association. But by 1946, Hospital Care decided to discontinue its medical benefit program for two reasons. First, the rate structure had proven inadequate, and second, the companion liability for Blue Cross hospitalization had decidedly increased because of the medical benefit.[11] Although its charter remained intact, the Medical Service Association had no members or income shortly after the war concluded.

In 1946, two significant developments in the health service prepayment movement occurred

Did You Know?

The now-familiar Blue Shield symbol was devised in 1939 by Carl Metzger of the Plan in Buffalo, New York. He wanted the design for the new medical service Plan to be linked to the companion hospital Plans, which were represented by the Blue Cross symbol, yet still distinctive. The serpent image in the center of the shield is associated with Aesculapius, the physician in Greek mythology. His snake-entwined staff represents healing and the renewal of life. This Greek image was combined with the insignia of the U.S. Army Medical Corps to create the now familiar Blue Shield. Metzger and his colleagues freely shared the Blue Shield symbol with other Plans like Hospital Care and Hospital Saving (predecessors of Blue Cross and Blue Shield of North Carolina), infusing the medical prepayment movement with a wider sense of identity long before there was a national Blue Shield organization. Approved Blue Shield Plans were not authorized to use the emblem until 1947.[12]

The Hospital Saving Association received approval as an official Blue Shield Plan in 1947 and was among the first 17 Plans authorized to use the Blue Shield emblem. Photo courtesy of the BCBSA archives.

on the national level. First, the Blue Cross Commission, the early national organization of Blue Cross Plans, was created. Second, the formation of Associated Medical Care Plans (AMCP), the first national organization of Blue Shield Plans, quickly followed in 1947. The AMCP was set up as a subsidiary of the American Medical Association's Council on Medical Service to help with the approval and coordination processes and to provide advice to Blue Shield Plans. By this point, AMA and prepayment leaders recognized that the proliferation of independent, local plans was not the best path. There needed to be increasing attention to national development and coordination as well.[13] The Hospital Saving Association received approval as an official Blue Shield Plan in 1947, and was among the first 17 Plans authorized to use the Blue Shield emblem (see *Did You Know?*). Its approval hinged, in part, on its sponsorship by the state's Medical Society, which Hospital Care did not have, delaying its approval as a Blue Shield Plan until 1962.

Given the devastation caused by the state's recurrent polio epidemics, both Hospital Care and Hospital Saving began offering new comprehensive certificates that covered the full cost of ward care as well as special riders for "dread diseases"

such as polio, diphtheria, and smallpox. Hospital Saving also added "dread disease" and extended benefits riders to its programs in 1949. These laid the groundwork for Blue Cross and Blue Shield of North Carolina's later major medical program. A frightened public quickly sought the protection of the inexpensive riders, which cost only $2 for an individual and $5 per family for up to $6,000 in additional coverage.

As health insurance was reaching more of the state and the nation, the Hospital Care and Hospital Saving Associations were realizing the public service vision of their founders. More and more people were joining the Plans and enjoying the security of coverage, but hospital and medical costs were rising even faster. As the 1940s drew to a close, both Blue Plans were experimenting with innovative cost containment measures. Hospital Saving introduced the new idea of coinsurance to its subscribers in 1948. As Bill Houck, former Hospital Saving salesman, explained, "We had to have either more money or fewer benefits. So we guessed that people would not mind paying the first $5 copayment. It went over like a lead balloon. People didn't like the idea of having to pay this small amount, so they chose instead to keep their benefits and pay a higher rate."[14]

1949

Infant mortality rates decline 52 percent from 1930 through 1949, thanks to the availability of antibiotics and childhood immunizations, greater access to health care, and technological advances in maternal and neonatal medicine.

In 1949, the last N.C. county yet to do so establishes a full-time health department.

The controversial *Kinsey Reports,* published between 1948 and 1953, scientifically describe human sexual behavior and reach best-seller status.

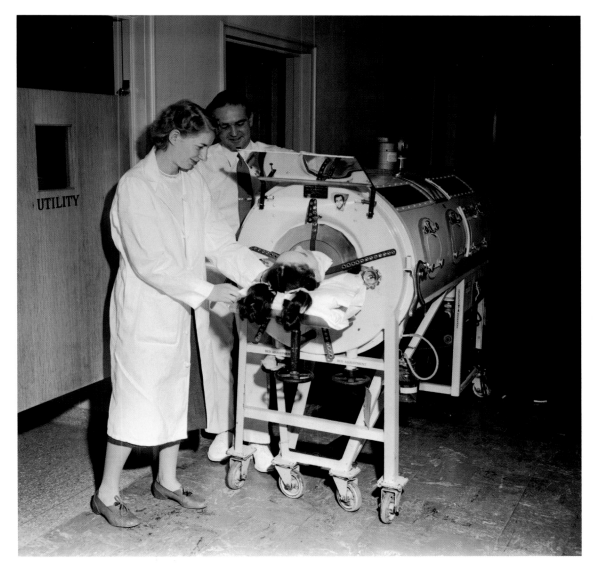

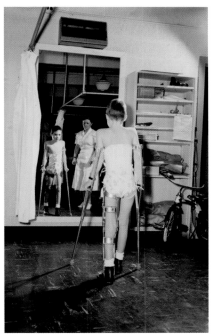

N.C. Blue Plans began offering additional coverage for polio to help families gain access to respiratory treatment with the iron lung device and afford medical equipment, such as braces and crutches. Photos courtesy of the North Carolina Collection, University of North Carolina at Chapel Hill. Brochure courtesy of the BCBSNC archives.

POLIO
PROTECTION

YOU CANNOT AFFORD TO BE WITHOUT

BENEFITS UP TO $6,000.00

FOR EACH AFFLICTED PERSON

For the Following Services, as Needed Within Three Years After Contracting Polio.

- Hospital Board and Room and General Nursing Services.
- Necessary Miscellaneous Hospital Expenses, Including Drugs, Medicines, Use of Orthopedic Appliances or Other Hospital Equipment and Physiotherapy.
- Use or Rental of Iron Lung While in Hospital.
- Services of Private Duty Nurses While in Hospital.
- Services of Licensed Physicians (in or out of Hospital).

- Ambulance Service to and from Hospital.
- Covers You and All Members of Your Family who are Eligible for Benefits Under Your Membership Certificate.

AVAILABLE AS RIDER ONLY TO MEMBERS OF

HOSPITAL SAVING ASSOCIATION
(Blue Cross—Blue Shield)

RATES PER YEAR	
ONE-PERSON	$2.00
TWO-PERSON	$4.00
FAMILY	$5.00

Hospital Saving Association
Blue Cross—Blue Shield
Chapel Hill, N. C.

People began to travel again freely during the postwar years, creating a need for health insurance benefits that could be used away from home. Photo courtesy of the BCBSNC archives.

Now ANOTHER GREAT ALL NEW SERVICE FOR BLUE CROSS SUBSCRIBERS

BLUE CROSS INTER-PLAN SERVICE BENEFIT BANK

PROVIDES SERVICE BENEFITS WHEN HOSPITALIZED

Away from Home

Increasingly, Hospital Care leader E. M. Herndon recognized how unlikely it would be for any nonprofit to successfully meet the minimum full costs of hospitalizations. The Plan had to factor in the different types of hospitals (teaching, public, and private), as well as different accounting methods and rate schedules. As a result, there was no standard by which adequate and fair costs could be determined by the prepayment plans. One solution was the idea of nationwide standardization of hospital accounting and cost procedures, which was one of several trends developing on the national level.

America's postwar economy was changing in several ways that helped shape the development of health service prepayment plans. More and more large industrial employers were building new plants in multiple locations across the country. At the same time, unionized labor had gained a strong negotiating position for health benefits with the passage of the Taft-Hartley Act in 1947. Corporate and union leaders agreed on the need for more national uniformity of coverage. A few trial syndicates even tried to compete with commercial carriers for such national accounts. But uniformity of benefits was hard to achieve given that there were not yet any national account contracts developed among Blue Cross and Blue Shield Plans.

The American public was also indulging in more long-distance automobile travel, since gasoline was again plentiful after the war years. This trend, coupled with the technological advances in medical care delivery, resulted in patients sometimes receiving treatment at regional medical centers or teaching hospitals across state lines. To address this trend, in 1949 the national Blue Cross organization developed a reciprocity arrangement known as the Inter-Plan Service Benefit Bank. In this arrangement, a Plan could purchase service from the "bank" so that its subscribers could receive care anywhere in the country at their "home" rates.[15] Hospital Care and Hospital Saving both voted to participate in the Inter-Plan Service Benefit Bank that year. Similarly, Hospital Saving developed its own ad hoc reciprocity arrangement for a while with the Plan in Richmond, Virginia.

Merger Talks: Round Two

As both Hospital Care and Hospital Saving struggled to keep pace with intense demands —membership growth, increasing costs on many fronts, competition with each other and with commercial carriers—interest in the idea of merging the two Associations resumed. Committees from the two Associations met and developed a working plan for a merger in 1946. The proposal for combining the two boards suggested that the new governing body include four doctors, four hospital administrators, and eight public representatives. Hospital Saving accepted the proposed structure, but Hospital Care declined, insisting that the new board should have more experienced membership in

its formative years—six doctors, six hospitals, and six public representatives. Hospital Saving balked at this counterproposal, believing that it would give Hospital Care a dominant presence on the board. As talks continued into the 1950s, compromise remained elusive.

The 1940s had been marked by wartime restrictions, renewed debate over national health care, and astounding growth in health insurance coverage in North Carolina and nationwide. The Blue Shield had arrived, enabling the state's hospital prepayment plans to expand their mission to improve access to health care by offering new medical and surgical prepayment services. When a series of polio epidemics hit the state, particularly its children, the Hospital Care and Hospital Saving Associations responded quickly, offering special coverage to help families get the care they needed. Thanks to the statewide Good Health campaign and Hill-Burton legislation, the health status of North Carolinians began to improve as more physicians were recruited, more hospitals were built, and more people recognized the value of health insurance. The decade concluded in North Carolina with experiments in cost containment and another failed merger attempt between Hospital Care and Hospital Saving. Both merger considerations and escalating health care costs would continue to inform the business development of the state's two nonprofit Blue Cross and Blue Shield Plans for years to come, but their commitment to the health of North Carolina's people would never waver.

Chapter Three

Growing Pains

Postwar Prosperity

Americans were enjoying a newfound prosperity following World War II. Once wartime wage and price controls were lifted, both income and spending soared. GIs returned and filled colleges and universities. Suburban neighborhoods began to flourish, and the "baby boom" swelled the U.S. population.

Health care became the fastest-growing sector in the unleashed postwar economy. Health insurance was now reaching 58 percent of all Americans, providing them access to medical care and timely hospitalization that was better and more affordable than ever before. Patient outcomes were dramatically improving through research, the development of new medicines and technology, and a stronger infrastructure, including the expansion of the National Institutes of Health. Infectious diseases such as polio, which had ravaged thousands, slowly began to be eradicated through the discovery of new vaccines,

widespread inoculation efforts, and the development of a new "iron lung" device.[1] The spread of the longtime killer tuberculosis, too, was substantially slowed by successful new antibiotic treatments.

In North Carolina, the Good Health Campaign, the availability of funding from the Hill-Burton program, and support from the Duke Endowment had a profoundly positive impact on the health of the state's citizens and the availability of health care providers and facilities.

The annual birth rate in the United States soared during the post–World War II era. By the time of the "baby boom," the majority of Americans had voluntary health insurance, and health care first became the fastest-growing sector of the economy. Photo courtesy of Watts Hospital archives.

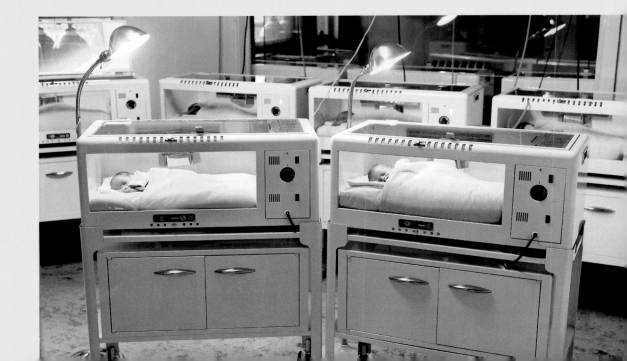

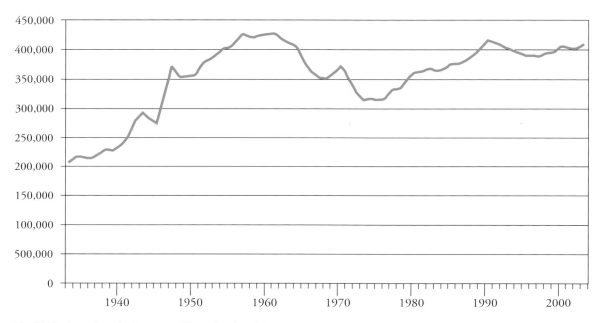

The "baby boom" peaked in 1957. Chart developed from U.S. Census data on live births.

Both the Hospital Care and Hospital Saving Associations had developed and vigorously promoted "dread disease" riders in the early 1950s to provide coverage of illnesses such as polio. But within a few years they were barely selling because effective treatments had been developed. By 1955, the Hospital Care Association offered its polio and "dread disease" rider at no additional charge to its members, since claims had dropped dramatically.[2] Between 1946 and 1956, the number of hospitals in the state increased by more than 16 percent. Six thousand new hospital beds had been added since 1946, an increase of nearly 33 percent, ranking North Carolina fourth in the nation.[3] More than a quarter million North Carolinians now had health insurance coverage through the growing Blue Plans. The state's health status was clearly on the rise.

In 1951, a record high 58 percent of all Americans had voluntary health insurance, fueling increased utilization of hospital and medical services. Following the national trend, membership growth in North Carolina's two Blue Cross and Blue Shield Plans was explosive. The Hospital Saving Association showed a 40 percent increase in enrollment in 1950 over the previous year. Between 1946 and 1956, the combined

In 1950, the average life expectancy in the United States is 68.2 years. In North Carolina, the numbers are worse: 66.5 years for white males, and only 58.5 for nonwhite males. White women fare better, living until age 72.9, but nonwhite women are only expected to live 62.8 years.

In 1950, President Harry Truman signs the Social Security Amendments, known as "Old-Age Assistance"; they will serve as the foundation for the future Medicaid program.

Cornerstone Of State-Wide Plan

The North Carolina Good Health Program Is Reaching Maturity

By ROBERT W. MADRY

Chapel Hill—After struggling through growing pains for half a dozen years, the North Carolina Good Health Program has finally reached the stage of adolescence and seems well along the way to maturity.

Five years ago there were 33 counties in North Carolina without a hospital bed. Today the number has been cut to 17.

A total of 104 projects looking toward a healthier North Carolina have been initiated since the program was activated in 1947. They involve a budget of $60,-000,000.

Forty-four of the projects have been completed, 46 are under construction, and 14 are projected. The State's hospital facilities have been increased by about one-third.

Under the program set up in 1947 a total of 39 new hospitals were to be built, but that doesn't begin to tell the whole story, for substantial additions were provided for 29 of the existing hospitals to bring the total to 68 with 4,287 beds.

When this program is completed, no citizen in North Carolina will be more than an hour's driving distance from one of these hospitals.

Fifteen health centers were in the plan, and five of these have already been completed. Of 15 nursing homes approved, nine have been completed and six are under construction. The 15 nursing homes will give the State an additional 1,013 beds.

Added up, this means that North Carolina now ranks second in the nation in post-war hospital construction. Figures from the U. S. Public Health Service include work under contract last July 1 and show that Texas leads with 5,176 beds, followed by North Carolina with 4,-287. Other states next in order are Ohio, New York, Pennsylvania and New Jersey.

Great Increase In Hospital Beds

North Carolina has had a phenomenal increase in hospital beds in the last quarter of the century. In 1924 there were 2,-186, in 1947 9,635. The number now is estimated at 14,000.

The size of the hospitals range from 20-bed institutions such as those at Bryson City, Sparta and Belhaven to the 400-bed teaching hospital being constructed at Chapel Hill in conjunction with the University's expanded four-year medical school. Seven of the plants have a hundred beds or more.

Dr. John A. Farrell, executive secretary of the North Carolina Medical Care Commission, points out that only a third of the burden of the total new program has been borne by the State.

In round figures, the program, as of July, had cost more than $60,000,000 approximately one-third of which was appropriated respectively by the State, and the cities and counties of North Carolina.

Under the plans it is the responsibility of the University of North Carolina's Health Center at Chapel Hill to serve as the cornerstone for the coordinated State-wide program.

A report just issued by Dr. Henry T. Clark, Jr., administrator of the recently created Division of Health Affairs, presents an amazing picture of progress at the Health Center during the last academic year.

At the University here, Dr. Clark's report emphasizes, a large, complicated, and in many respects unique Health Center, is growing from relatively humble beginnings.

"Approximately 85 percent of the proposed construction for the Health Center is now committed to contracts, and the State Budget Bureau has authorized the transfer of certain financial reserves which will cover remaining essential needs," the report says.

New Medical Facilities

Planning and construction of new medical facilities made steady progress during the academic year 1950-51. The main 400-bed teaching hospital and out-patient clinic, on which construction was begun in October, 1949, are now 75 per cent completed despite a strike during the past winter. This building should be turned over to the University by January, 1952, and be ready for acceptance of patients by the following April.

In August, 1950, the contract was let for a cancer research floor in the clinic building, for which the U. S. Public Health Service contributed $200,000, and this floor will be completed at the same time as the main hospital and clinic building.

Construction of dormitory quarters for approximately 100 interns, residents and fellows was started in November, 1950, and this building should be ready for use by June, 1952.

Contracts were let last March for a North "wing" to the main medical building to provide necessary increased teaching and research facilities for the Departments of Pathology, Anatomy and Pharmacology. Plans are now underway for a comparable South "wing" which will be started by October.

Since the main offices of the School of Public Health occupy the ground floor of this same building, the "wing" construction will also provide some space relief for that School.

In July a contract was let for converting the top floor of the present infirmary (which is, in effect, a wing of the main hospital) into an obstetrical floor and for the addition of another floor to complete the obstetrical-gynecological in-patient facilities.

TB and Psychiatry Units

In addition to these construction projects, action by the 1951 General Assembly provided for two more key units for the total Health Center. In the field of tuberculosis, funds were appropriated by the Legislators of 1949 and 1951 to the North Carolina Sanatorium Board of Directors to construct a 100-bed chest unit adjacent to the main University hospital. The Federal government also appropriated

MUCH PROGRESS IS BEING MADE in the construction of the Teaching Hospital and four-year Medical School at the University of North Carolina in Chapel Hill. The building is scheduled for completion by the first of the year and for formal opening in April. Here is a front view showing the present stage of construction of the handsome building which adjoins the present Medical School and Infirmary.

western School of Medicine, as Professor of Medicine.

The regular basic science teaching program in the Medical School functioned at an increased tempo during 1950-51 since instruction of the first class of dental students was added to the usual teaching load.

This Fall 58 highly promising students, a maximum class, have been accepted for the first-year class in medicine.

In the field of research, the basic science faculty has been as active as heavy teaching programs, cramped quarters and small budgets permitted. As one indication of activity, however, there were 57 publications from the various departments during the year and modest "outside" grants of over $100,000 for 17 individual projects.

In the field of service, the Department of Pathology deserves

in expendable funds and the eventual building of a multimillion dollar endowment. During its first full year of operation, the goal for expendable funds was passed and progress was made on the endowment.

School Of Dentistry

The School of Dentistry proved its vigor by accepting its first class of 40 students last Fall, by conducting its instruction program largely in Quonset huts, and by developing what one faculty member described as "the finest group spirit in my 25 years of dental instruction." The arrival of a second class this month has created even greater space problems but these are being met on an improvised basis.

Adequate facilities for dental instruction await the completion of the "wings" to the Medical building (for basic science instruction) and the School of Dentistry building itself (for clinical instruction). Construction of the

An integrated four-year program of nursing education, with admission of freshmen women students, was approved by the Board of Trustees last March.

addition, 1,300 other non-degree students received instruction from public health faculty members in the regular courses, in institutes and in field training areas.

The School now has 76 full-time staff members, including 31 full-time faculty members, engaged in vital teaching, research and service work.

Of the total operating budget of $500,000, only about $200,000 represented State appropriations. In addition, approximately $100,-000 represented teaching grants from private and governmental agencies, and the remaining large sum represented research grants.

School Of Pharmacy

The most noteworthy items during the year in the well-established School of Pharmacy were the promotion of Prof. Edward Brecht to the Deanship

In 1952, the polio epidemic peaked in the United States and in North Carolina. The Salk injectable polio vaccine was developed in 1953. Schoolchildren, shown here waiting in segregated lines, were vaccinated by the thousands, which led to an almost 90 percent drop in the disease within two years. Photo courtesy of the Memphis Commercial Appeal.

membership of the Hospital Care and Hospital Saving Associations tripled. Both Associations rapidly expanded their staffs and outgrew their early offices. In 1951, Hospital Saving moved to its West Franklin Street headquarters in Chapel Hill, where it remained until consolidation. Likewise, Hospital Care moved to larger quarters at 420 West Geer Street in Durham (see *Did You Know?*).

But the rapid growth trends in both insurance plan membership and utilization of services were accompanied by a dramatic upsurge in health care costs. Hospital rates tripled, escalating at a pace far greater than that of doctors' fees or the price of drugs. For example, in 1955 the Hospital Care Association reported a 15 percent increase in payments to doctors and hospitals over the previous year. Hospital Saving's average daily hospital charge was now $18, and it held little more than a month's operating reserves. With more Americans accessing health care services and paying for them through health insurance, young Blue Plans such as those in North Carolina were now confronted with managing an increasingly complex equation of providers and patients, contracts and costs. Plan leaders, including Hospital Saving's Eugene B.

Crawford, puzzled over why North Carolinians were being admitted to hospitals with more frequency than the national average. Was there abuse of the coverage, or were the state's citizens just not as healthy? The simple community service mission upon which the Blue prepayment plans were founded was no longer so simple to administer.

Changing Consumer Demand and Fierce Competition

One answer lay in the rising expectations of health care consumers. In the new economy of the 1950s, purchasers of health care insurance were demanding more comprehensive benefit packages. Even with the remarkable growth experienced by Blue Plans across the nation during the post–World War II era, commercial indemnity plans enjoyed the most rapid expansion overall of any type of health insurance, doubling the number of their subscribers from 1945 to 1949. In a show of some territoriality, Hospital Care Association's Rural Enrollment Director, Ruth Wanzer, reported that tempers were flaring among her subscribers over the superabundance of mail being received from out-of-state hospital

1950　　　　　　　　　**1951**

Two studies linking smoking to lung cancer are published in 1950 in a prominent medical journal. Public debate about the health consequences of smoking intensifies, and North Carolina's thriving tobacco industry challenges the connection.

By 1951, a record high 58 percent of all Americans have voluntary health insurance, fueling increased utilization of hospital and medical services. In North Carolina, the Hospital Care Association insures over a quarter million members.

Rabies is a major problem in North Carolina as well as much of the rest of the nation during the 1950s. Despite the availability of a rabies vaccine, many people still rely on natural remedies such as a "madstone."

insurance companies. This alarming competitive trend was continuing during the early 1950s, as commercial carriers developed attractive package plans that they could administer nationwide far more easily than through the fragmented, localized Blue Plans, who found it difficult to offer consistent coverage across state lines.

Large employers with branches in several states were sometimes bewildered by having to deal with up to 50 different Blue Plans to cover their employees. This problem had been mitigated by the practice of having the Plan in the state in which the company had its headquarters act as a broker that would then deal with other Plans. The 1950 agreement between U.S. Steel and Blue Cross of Western Pennsylvania was a landmark agreement in which 900,000 workers and their families nationwide would be covered by a single contract. Similarly, in North Carolina, the Hospital Saving Association acted as the broker for Piedmont Airlines, which was headquartered in Winston-Salem but had seven different Blue Cross Plans in five states covering its employees. Later in 1950, the national Blue Cross Association established a new agency, Health Service, Inc., to act as a single national Blue Cross contract source for the provision of uniform coverage for large

national accounts and to manage the complexity of multi-Plan coverage.[5]

Labor unions were another major influence on the health insurance market. Although the 1947 Taft-Hartley Act was far less favorable toward unions than the previous National Labor Relations Act had been, it still protected labor's ability to engage in collective bargaining agreements about the terms of employment, including health and pension benefits. In 1954, unions counted for 25 percent of all health insurance and were demanding large employer contributions to their health benefits packages. As a result, major industrial accounts had tremendous power in their contract negotiations for insurance coverage, as they were easily able to foment competition for their business between the Blue Plans and commercial carriers. E. M. Herndon, former president of the Hospital Care Association, captured the essence of the challenge when he wrote: "Being a nonprofit organization, Blue Cross is in a position to better serve the health needs of the community than commercial insurance companies, but Blue Cross must gain more nationwide cooperation without sacrificing its community service aspect, if it is to meet the competition."[6]

Contrary to the advertising messages widely promoted by the tobacco industry, research studies first linked smoking to lung cancer in 1950. Photo courtesy of the National Museum of American History.

Form 905

In fact, both Associations in North Carolina attempted to expand their markets beyond the now traditional hospital and medical prepayment options by offering life and disability coverage packages. In 1953, the Hospital Care Association formed Group Insurance Service (GIS), and in 1954, Hospital Saving organized HSA Insurance Services, Inc. These kinds of group-life programs proved attractive to the thousands of federal government employees, and a syndicate led by Metropolitan Life, a commercial carrier, rapidly enrolled the majority of them—another lost opportunity for Blue Plans overall.[7]

Although the Hospital Care and Hospital Saving Associations remained the market leaders in North Carolina, they realized that the competitive field was expanding beyond their traditional rivalry with each other. If Blue Plans were to remain competitive, they would need to find a way to act as a system that could offer uniform benefits at uniform rates nationwide, and to administer fast, efficient claims service regardless of where the subscriber received medical attention. In the 1950s, they had not yet found a way to relinquish some of their grassroots approaches in order to thrive on a coordinated national level.

Or was it that Plans were simply not yet willing to cooperate with one another? The pattern of failed merger attempts over the previous 17 years between the Hospital Care and Hospital Saving Associations certainly underlines the triumph of competition over cooperation. This pattern prevailed again in the 1950s. Early in 1950, the

Blue Cross Commission of the American Hospital Association tried to pressure the two North Carolina Plans into a merger. The Commission crafted an arbitration agreement and indicated that it would withhold official approval as Blue Cross Plans if one or both of the Plans refused to sign it. Essentially, an ultimatum had been issued. Representatives of both Associations quickly consulted with the state commissioner of insurance and the assistant attorney general, who issued an opinion that the proposed agreement would actually be contrary to the state statutes under which the Plans operated.

A merger had once again been averted. Even so, the Blue Cross Commission and others continued to agitate for consolidation. By 1955, Hospital Care and Hospital Saving were among only a few Blue Plans in the nation that competed with one another within the same geographic area. Since most Blue Cross Plans had exclusive districts, it was difficult for Blue Cross Commission leaders to understand how North Carolina's competing Plans could actually benefit their members. In 1955, a delegation including a representative from Hospital Care, Hospital Saving, and the Duke Endowment was dispatched to the Commission's Chicago headquarters to explain the situation and try to reduce this national pressure for consolidation.[8] They achieved a greater understanding and were able to continue operating independently—for better or worse.

The Ratings Dilemma

In addition to their lack of systemic coordination, another competitive disadvantage was the Blue Plans' use of "community rating." This was the practice of offering the same rates to everyone in a given service area regardless of age, sex, or occupation, thus dividing the risk equally among members, regardless of the frequency of their hospitalizations. Hospital Care and Hospital Saving had used community rating since their inception in the 1930s, and it was regarded as fundamental to their service missions, since community rating was essentially democratic in nature, given that individuals were not discriminated against by health status.

In stark contrast, profit was central to the operations of the commercial insurance carriers. Instead of sharing the risk through community rating, they implemented "experience rating," in which rates were based on the actual loss

1952

The polio epidemic in the United States peaks in 1952, with 60,000 new cases reported.

A breakthrough in medical technology occurs with development of the first external cardiac pacemaker in 1952.

N.C. Memorial Hospital in Chapel Hill is completed in 1952 and opens the nation's first intensive care unit in 1953. Intensive care units are increasingly used for the treatment and continuous monitoring of seriously ill patients by skilled personnel using special techniques and medical technology.

1953

In 1953, Watson and Crick first accurately describe the double helix structure of DNA. Their discovery is regarded as the founding event of molecular biology and opens the door to new medical treatments and diagnostic tests for decades to come.

Did You Know?

As the Hospital Care Association continued to grow, it increasingly needed to use modern office equipment instead of employees using handwritten ledgers to process claims and capture enrollment information. In 1950, Hospital Care purchased new IBM punch card tabulating machines (a predecessor of computers) for this purpose. Although there was excitement about these new "mechanical brains" and the expected gains in efficiency, there was also serious concern about the stress that the weight of these heavy machines would put on the Association's current quarters, which were then located on an upper floor above the Guaranty State Bank on Durham's Market Street. Few people know that the move to the company's former West Geer Street location was prompted by a fear of collapsing floors![4]

experience of a given employee group. Many large industrial accounts preferred experience rating, as they objected to paying community rates to help subsidize groups with high losses. The commercial carriers recognized the opportunity to cherry-pick the biggest, healthiest groups from Blue Plans, leaving them to manage those groups with greater health risks. This trend contributed to Blue Plans' being regarded as "the insurer of last resort"—a distinction that protected many who would otherwise have had no coverage but was very costly to the Blues. While national Blue Cross leaders decried experience rating as "contrary to the community service ideal," they were confronted by the practical demands of changing consumer demands and competitive practices.

In the late 1940s, the Hospital Saving Association had experimented with "merit rating"—a form of experience rating in which a group with a favorable loss record could receive dividends in the form of lower membership fees if it built up sufficient reserves. But the state Insurance Commissioner objected to this practice because there was no legal provision for increasing dues again if that group's loss experience turned sour. As a result, merit rating was discontinued.[9]

Hospital Saving was also among the first Blue Plans in the nation to experiment with "cost-plus" arrangements, in which companies were essentially self-insured, with the Plan providing administrative services only (ASO).[10] Such ASO arrangements were provided for by the state statutes governing the operations of health service prepayment plans, and they continue today. The first cost-plus contract was with Hanes Hosiery, followed by R. J. Reynolds Tobacco Company, both major accounts for Hospital Saving in Winston-Salem.

But cost-plus service offerings were a peripheral part of the core coverage of North Carolina's prepayment plans and were no match for the lure of experience rating offered by commercial carriers. Hospital Care and Hospital Saving would have to find a way to resolve the tension between their community service ideals and the encroachment of for-profit competition on their once easy-to-enroll territories. They would have to work both sides of the equation—appeal to large accounts in the textile and tobacco industries and reach the still-underserved rural population of the state.

Expanding Markets

The rapid growth experienced by the state's prepayment plans in their first two decades of service had been driven by selling group coverage to large organizations. Unfortunately, this practice had inadvertently excluded many of those who needed health insurance the most from qualifying for it. Rural families with low or unpredictable seasonal incomes often did not belong to groups eligible for Blue Cross coverage, and too often they had to resort to purchasing inexpensive and often inadequate coverage

Rural families with low or unpredictable seasonal incomes often did not belong to groups eligible for health insurance. Photo courtesy of BCBSA archives.

from commercial carriers—or to going without insurance.

To combat this trend, Hospital Care began offering group rate coverage to any rural organization with five or more members. In 1953, Hospital Care launched a new rural group enrollment campaign with the Farmer's Federation Cooperative in 20 counties in western North Carolina, one of the poorest areas of the state. A rural group enrollment department was also established, and more than 500 volunteer workers from across the state were recruited and trained to assist in reaching the widely dispersed rural population. These efforts resulted in eligibility for many rural groups, including Farm Bureaus, Granges, home demonstration clubs, civic groups, churches, and landowners with tenants. Hospital Care Association promoted this new opportunity in many ways at events and in communities across the state. In 1954, Hospital Care Blue Cross displays could be seen at county fairs, the state Public Health Conference, and the American Federation of Labor's annual meeting. The Duke Endowment also recognized the needs of the state's underserved rural population. In 1955, it made a grant of $6,000 to help finance a new program for low-income rural families.

The Hospital Care Association put up matching funds and conducted successful enrollment drives in Bladen and Iredell Counties. By 1959, Hospital Care attributed the majority of its growth to rural enrollment.

In addition, Hospital Care inaugurated intensive nongroup enrollment campaigns on a semiannual basis. For a limited period, individuals under 65 years old, whether they were self-employed or unemployed, could sign up for a standard certificate. This open enrollment period was highly publicized in hospitals, doctors' offices, and drugstores, and even on city buses, in an effort to reach as many uninsured North Carolinians as possible.

The health care needs of the poor and elderly were also coming into the spotlight on the federal and state levels. In 1950, President Harry Truman signed the Social Security Amendments, called "Old-Age Assistance," which provided federal funds to states for vendor payments for medical care of the aged living at the poverty level. This assistance became the foundation for the future Medicaid program. Then in February 1952, Federal Security Administrator Oscar Ewing publicly proposed enactment of health insurance for Social Security beneficiaries. By December of

(facing) The trend toward hospital births was more prevalent among white, middle- to upper-class women. Cost and distance to the hospital deterred others. In rural areas, poor white and African American women often still relied on delivery by a midwife. Photo courtesy of Robert Galbraith.

1954

In 1954, labor unions count for 25 percent of all health insurance and are demanding large employer contributions to their health benefits packages.

In 1954, the U.S. Supreme Court rules segregation in the public schools illegal. At this time, only 13 hospitals are serving the needs of the African American population in North Carolina. With desegregation, their access to health care greatly improves, and the trend toward giving more black doctors medical and surgical privileges at hospitals accelerates.

In 1954, the first truly successful kidney transplant is performed from one twin to another without any immunosuppressive medication.

1955

Jonas Salk's polio vaccine is licensed in 1955 and is used in a mass vaccination of nearly 2 million schoolchildren in the United States. Albert Sabin develops a safe oral vaccine in 1957. The incidence of polio in United States falls by 85–90 percent between 1955 and 1957.

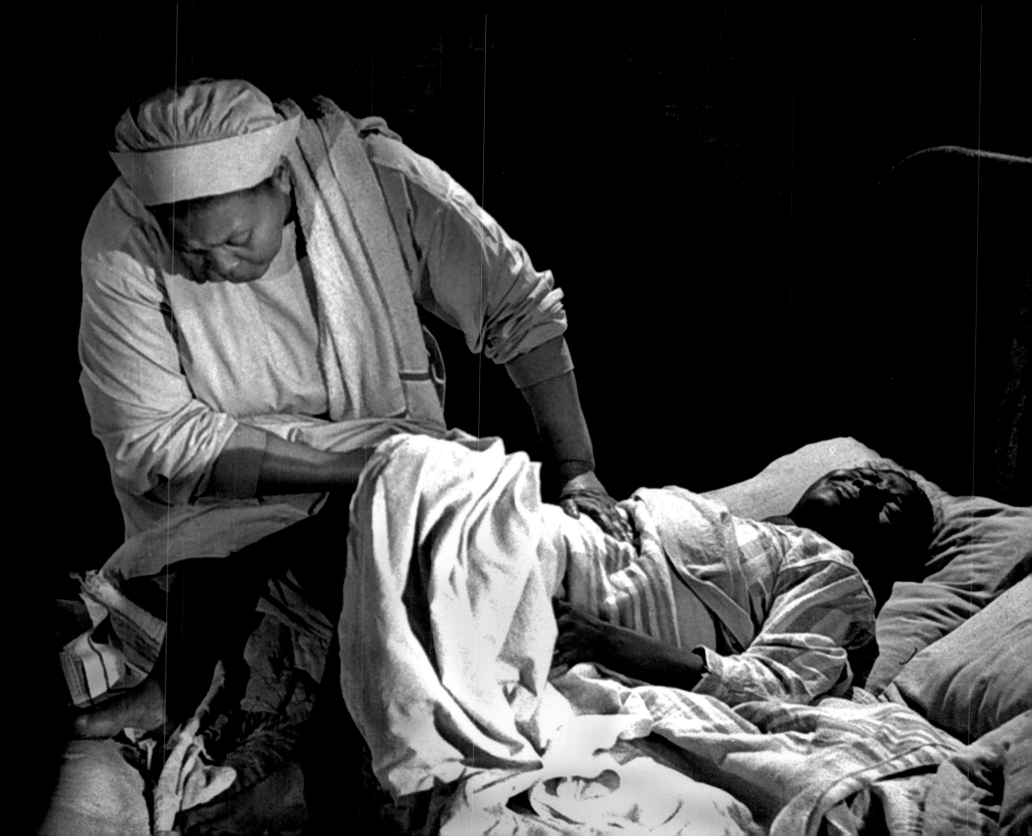

that year, President Truman's Commission on the Health Needs of the Nation endorsed the idea.[11]

But as previous history had shown, moves toward a national health insurance program tended to meet with highly polarized, partisan responses. Democrats regularly attempted to find ways to offer health coverage to all Americans, with particular attention to the needs of those with low access to health services, while Republicans offered vigorous opposition to what they and the AMA constituency viewed as "socialized medicine." With the election of Republican President Dwight Eisenhower in 1952, the possibility of passing any compulsory national health insurance effectively ended during his two terms in office.

Agreement about low-income programs was also difficult to reach on a state level. But after considerable controversy over fee schedules, the North Carolina Medical Society agreed in 1952 to the provisions of a new "Doctors Program" that guaranteed payment of certain medical services in full for low-income families, in cooperation with the Hospital Saving Association as payor. Every licensed white physician in North Carolina was given an opportunity to participate in the program, and more than 50 percent of them

signed participating agreements. In a significant concession toward racial inclusion, the Medical Society authorized Hospital Saving to also accept participating agreements from licensed black physicians.[12] Given that there were 13 hospitals serving the state's African American community at this time, access to care began to improve significantly. Only two years later, in 1954, segregation in the public schools was declared illegal by the U.S. Supreme Court in *Brown v. Board of Education,* and over the next several years other Supreme Court decisions and repeals of state and federal pro-segregation laws began to move the country toward further racial integration. These changes opened the way for black physicians to get admitting privileges at more hospitals and for patients to have many more ways to receive high-quality health care.

New Opportunities with the Federal Government

Eisenhower came to office as the illustrious commanding general from World War II, who then obtained a truce in the Korean War during his administration. As president, Eisenhower favored programs for veterans and their families, while

In 1954, North Carolina had only 13 hospitals serving the health care needs of African Americans. That same year the landmark Supreme Court decision to desegregate public schools paved the way for integration in other institutions, such as health care facilities. Photo courtesy of the Southern Historical Collection, Wilson Library, the University of North Carolina at Chapel Hill.

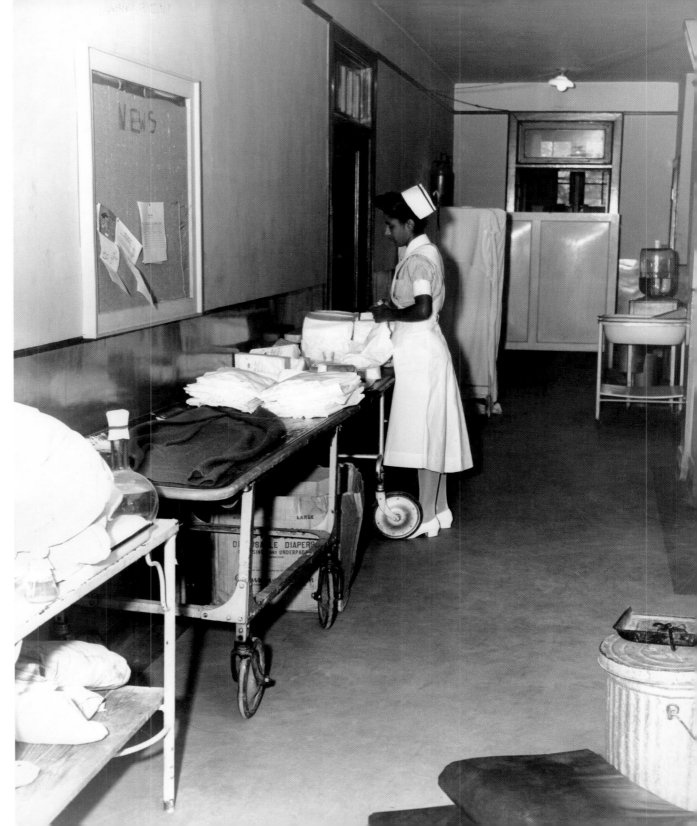

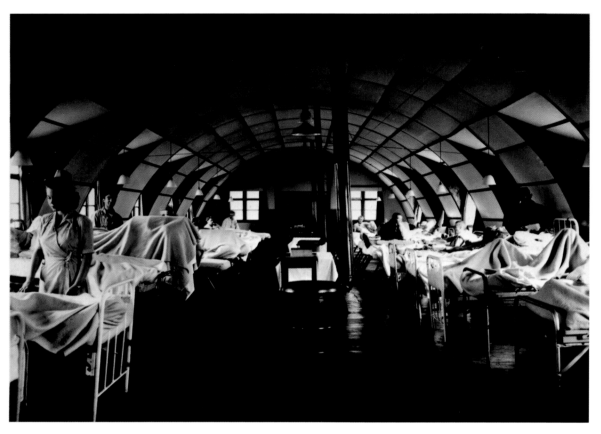

In 1956 the federal CHAMPUS program began providing military families the option of receiving medical care from civilian providers. N.C. Blue Plans cooperatively administered the program for thousands stationed at the state's military bases. Photo courtesy of Duke University Medical Archives.

continuing to oppose national health insurance. Both World War II and the Korean conflict had strained the capabilities of the military health care system. Hospital Saving seized the opportunity to become the first health service plan in the country to contract with the federal government to administer health care benefits for veterans. That program continued until 1960 and was administered on a cost-plus basis. Hospital Saving paid the claims and then charged the government directly for the cost of administering the program.

On Dec. 7, 1956, President Eisenhower also signed into law the Dependents Medical Care Act, which entitled all military dependents to medical care. Previously, military dependents had been able to receive care only at military bases when it was available, which resulted in inconsistent access to health care during and after wartime. This program was first known as "Medicare," but later amendments led to it being renamed the Civilian Health and Medical Program of the Uniformed Services (CHAMPUS). For the first time, the U.S. Defense Department contracted directly with the national Blue Cross Association (BCA) for the administration of CHAMPUS. The BCA then subcontracted with Blue Plans near military bases.

Between the Army at Fort Bragg, the Marines at Camp Lejeune and Cherry Point, and the Air Force at Pope and Seymour Johnson bases, North Carolina was home to more than 8,000 military dependents, so the state was a prime beneficiary of this new contract opportunity. Initially, both of North Carolina's Blue Plans cooperatively administered the program. But by 1958, the Hospital Care Association realized that it would be more efficient if only one of the two Plans processed the claims, and the Hospital Saving Association then became the sole service provider for the program. Medical care for returning soldiers also improved as the number of Veterans Administration (VA) hospitals grew to almost 100, and facilities began to be built in urban areas where they could be affiliated with medical schools and research institutions. Durham's VA hospital followed this pattern, opening in 1953 close to Duke University's School of Medicine.[13]

President Eisenhower also oversaw significant progress in services for the disabled. By the 1950s, Social Security had become a widely popular program with broad bipartisan support. Social Security Disability Insurance, by way of contrast, remained a controversial measure. In 1952 and 1954, vocational rehabilitation legislation was passed to help the disabled return to work, with states making the initial determinations of disability—a feature of the program that remains in place today. In 1955, the House once again passed a disability insurance measure, and

in 1956 the Senate Finance Committee again opposed it. A dramatic fight ensued on the floor of the Senate that resulted in the passage, by the barest of margins, of Social Security Disability Insurance (SSDI). In a significant expansion of Social Security benefits, President Eisenhower then signed the disability insurance program into law. The Hill-Burton hospital construction program was also expanded to cover rehabilitation facilities.

Given the high enrollment in group-life insurance among employees of the federal government, unions of federal workers began to pressure government leaders to further expand their benefit packages by including health insurance. In 1957, a proposal for group major medical indemnity insurance for federal employees was put forth by a group of commercial carriers. The stakes were tremendous, and national Blue Cross leaders argued fiercely that their service benefits would be far superior to the commercial indemnity coverage under consideration. The task of developing a rate and benefits package that 131 heterogeneous Plans could deliver at the agreed-upon price without knowing how many people would enroll was a high-risk venture that would require greater conformity than ever before. But

1955

1956

In the mid-1950s, closed chest defibrillators are first developed in the USSR and are later refined by NASA in the United States.

The era of using chemotherapy for cancer treatment begins in 1956, with the first cure of metastatic cancer using methotrexate.

In 1956, hospital stays of up to a week are typical for deliveries, even for normal births.

The annual birth rate in the United States surpasses 4 million for the first time in 1954, compared to 2 million at the close of the lean 1930s. The "baby boom" peaks in 1957, driving utilization of hospital and medical services for decades to come.

the risk of losing a share in the pool of over 2 million federal employees and their dependents was even greater. Legislators and Blue Cross negotiators engaged in extended discussions of the framework for an acceptable program over a torturous two years.[14]

Finally, in 1959 President Eisenhower signed into law the Federal Employee Health Benefits Program (known as FEP). The program of "controlled competition" offered government workers a choice between two different kinds of plans, such as Blue Cross and Blue Shield service benefit coverage or Aetna's commercial indemnity insurance. Once again, the contract was made between the government and the national Blue Cross Association, which then subcontracted with local Blue Plans. In North Carolina, more than 50,000 federal employees and their dependents became eligible for FEP coverage. Both the Hospital Care Association and Hospital Saving Association participated in underwriting the FEP in North Carolina and they continue to do so today. Of the federal employees who enrolled when FEP began, 54 percent chose Blue Cross and Blue Shield as their insurer of choice.[15] Both the CHAMPUS and FEP programs demonstrated that national

contracts with the federal government could be successfully administered through the Blue Cross Association in cooperation with local Plans.

Increased Cooperation in the Face of Competition

While the national Blue Cross Association was encouraging greater consistency and cooperation across Plans, North Carolina's Hospital Care and Hospital Saving Associations were developing new products and business practices in order to remain competitive and address their diminishing reserves. Despite their rivalry, they also found ways to cooperate. For example, in 1954 they had agreed to use identical agreements with contracting hospitals and a uniform hospital admission notice that carried the names of both Plans. The Associations also joined forces to sponsor various public service programs, including student nursing recruitment.

With the costs of hospitalization regularly outpacing the growth in membership, both Plans tried to avoid rate increases and instead offered new types of contracts and programs. Hospital Saving concentrated on promoting its extended benefits endorsement to counter the offerings

1958

1959

In 1958, the first successful human cardiac pacemaker is implanted.

In 1959, North Carolina becomes the first state in the nation to require polio vaccinations as a prerequisite for public school entry.

Health insurance coverage expands in North Carolina and the nation for both federal employees and senior citizens in 1959.

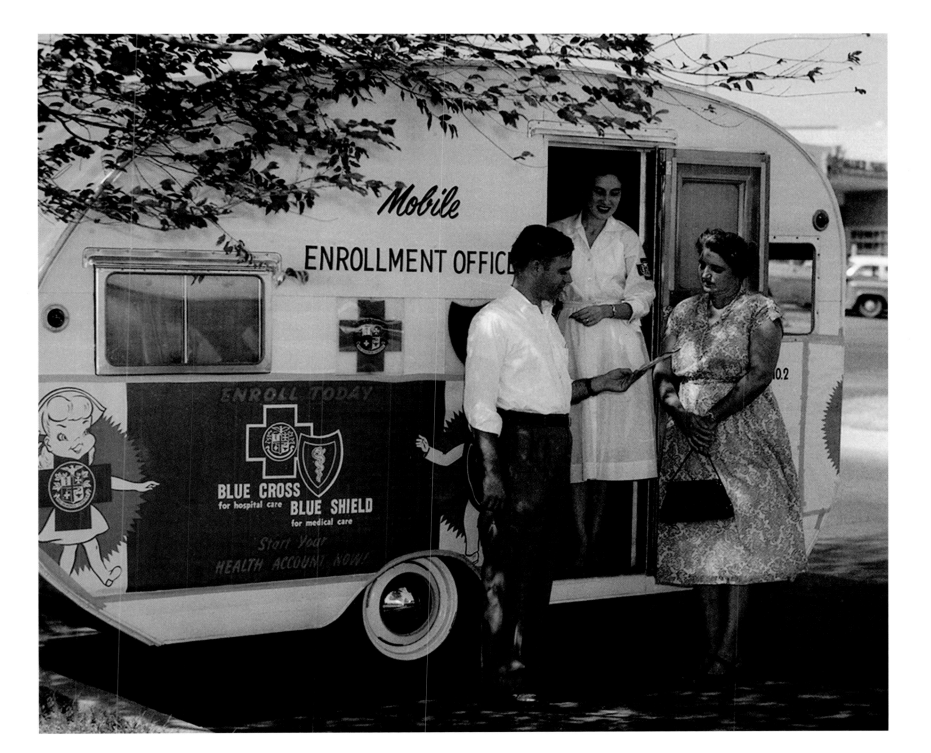

The first Blue Cross baby, Ann Woodard Reid, gave birth to her own Blue Cross baby in 1955. Hospital stays of up to a week following delivery were typical at that time for those with maternity benefits. Photo courtesy of BCBSA archives.

of commercial carriers. By 1958, Hospital Care followed suit with extended benefits and major medical endorsements to meet the increasing demand for catastrophic coverage. As the problem of inadequate health protection for the elderly entered the national spotlight at the end of the decade, Hospital Care for the first time in 1959 also offered a new senior citizen certificate to those over 65 in reasonably good health.

The reasons behind the overcrowding of North Carolina hospitals remained unclear, but the numbers were undeniable. In 1957, many of the state's leading hospitals were experiencing serious overcrowding. Raleigh's Rex Hospital was operating beyond capacity, with extra beds lining the halls on the medical and surgery floors. In Charlotte, Asheville, and Durham, the major hospitals were operating on a wait-list basis. The average number of Blue Cross admissions reported to the Hospital Care Association leaped from 1,500 to 2,000 weekly. As increasing hospital utilization continued to raise questions of abuse by members, hospitals, and doctors alike, both Plans began to scrutinize their underwriting practices more closely. In 1956, a statewide plan for auditing health care providers was initiated and eventually expanded to include review of hospital costs and charges. The Associations conducted workshops throughout the state to better inform participating hospitals, doctors, and the Plans. The reins were tightening, presaging the rigorous utilization review practices that decades later would characterize managed care.

Other aspects of leadership, strategy, and operations were changing inside the Associations as well. In 1954, the visionary founder and first president of the Hospital Saving Association, Dr. I. H. Manning, stepped down as chairman of the board, and P. Frank Hanes of the R. J. Reynolds Tobacco Company became the Association's new leader. While Manning had represented the significant influence of the state's medical community on the Plan's early development, Hanes's appointment marked an effort to include the perspectives of not only doctors and hospitals but also the public in board structure and decision making. Similarly, Dr. W. C. Davison, founder of the Hospital Care Association, retired from the board of directors in 1958.

The precipitous growth of both Associations had necessitated a significant expansion of staff and infrastructure. Technological advances were facilitating gains in efficiency of claims processing and other administrative functions. For example, in 1957 the Hospital Care Association became linked to 85 other Blue Cross Plans nationwide through a new private wire system. The wire system reduced the transmission time required for approval of out-of-state hospital admissions of its subscribers from 30 minutes to only 3, saving the Plan 60 percent of the costs

The origins of today's "Information Age" were visible in the large, costly computers first used during the 1950s to gain efficiency. Hospital Care began using this room-sized IBM computer in 1959 to process claims at what seemed like lightning speed compared to the manual ledgers and punch cards of preceding decades. Photo courtesy of IBM Corporation.

of sending approval notices. A dozen years after it was established, the IBM Department had become the largest in Hospital Care, surpassing the Benefits Department for the first time in 1959. As a room-sized IBM RAMAC computer was programmed to speed claims processing in the Benefits Department, questions about whether machines would replace employees began to surface nervously as early tremors of the "electronic age" were felt.[16]

The Hospital Care and Hospital Saving Associations were no longer fledgling Plans struggling to survive in a mostly rural state whose people suffered from poor health care and few health insurance options. In 1958, the Hospital Care Association was providing coverage to 325,000 members that represented the state's diverse population. Seniors and students, blacks and whites, farmers and factory workers now had improved access to physicians and hospitals statewide and help paying for their health care bills through N.C. Blue Plans. The first "Blue Cross baby," Ann Woodard Reid, had given birth to a child of her own in 1955, one of 18 million babies that had been delivered under the Blue Cross program since its inception. These were all reasons to celebrate as Hospital Care marked 25 years of helping improve the health of North Carolinians. At the turn of the decade, the Hospital Saving Association would also mark its silver anniversary. While both Associations celebrated their remarkable successes, they also faced serious business challenges as health care costs continued skyward, market demand became more sophisticated, and the competition both between the Blue Plans and from commercial carriers remained intense.

Chapter Four

From Cooperation to Consolidation

Health Insurance for the Poor and Elderly— A National Debate

From 1957 to 1965, the financing and delivery of health care to elderly and indigent populations was addressed primarily at the local rather than federal level. By 1959, North Carolina's Hospital Care Association was offering healthy applicants a new senior citizen certificate that quickly gained popularity. The Hospital Care and Hospital Saving Associations' "Easy Joining Days" campaigns also simplified enrollment requirements for many who had been previously ineligible to join. The Social Security Administration was allocating a small percentage of its funds to the aged and indigent through state and local welfare programs, but there remained no

comprehensive national program to address the mounting concern—a growing population of the elderly. While the federal government was slow to act on behalf of this vulnerable population, North Carolina's Blue Plans refused to wait. They continued to drive access to better health care by finding new ways to reach the underserved with health insurance coverage.

At the federal level, in 1958 Democratic politicians introduced the Forand bill, which included provisions for surgical insurance. The insurance feature particularly provoked the AMA lobby, but they had to be careful not to appear insensitive in their opposition.[1] The AMA's president, Dr. Louis M. Orr, decried the Forand bill as a "staggeringly expensive" solution that would lead to "poorer, not better" health care for the elderly,

The civil rights movement sought to end many types of discrimination in American society. In health care, it led to the integration of hospital staffs by allowing African American doctors to have medical and surgical privileges in formerly whites-only hospitals. Photo courtesy of the Southern Historical Collection, Wilson Library, the University of North Carolina at Chapel Hill.

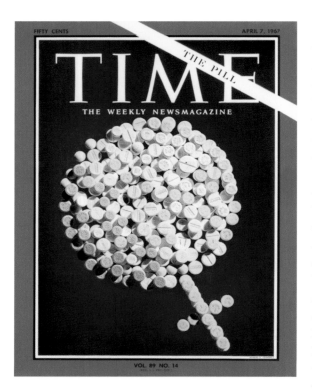

FIFTY CENTS

APRIL 7, 1967

TIME
THE WEEKLY NEWSMAGAZINE

THE PILL

VOL. 89 NO. 14

The development of the oral contraceptive in 1960 greatly expanded women's choices about their reproductive health and family planning. Photo courtesy of Time Inc.

result in "dangerously overcrowded" hospitals, and "eventually destroy the health insurance industry."[2] After its defeat, the Kerr-Mills bill put forward a plan that included medical assistance to "the medically indigent" elderly, which contributed to its passage in 1960. But the bill's impact was limited because it mandated matching funds from participating states.

The election of John F. Kennedy as president in 1960 marked the end of the conservatism that had characterized the 1950s and the onset of the comparatively experimental 1960s. Provision of health care for the elderly became part of the new administration's domestic agenda. Kennedy's program called for an expansion of Social Security benefits through increased Social Security taxes—a program that came to be known as "Medicare" and was introduced as the King-Anderson bill in 1961. Within the ranks of the national Blue Cross Association (BCA), there was strong disagreement about whether to back the King-Anderson bill. Some felt that the move represented "creeping socialism," while others felt the Blues should be pragmatic and present a reasonable alternative and, if all else failed, cooperate if a Social Security–based system passed (see *Did You Know?*).

As Hospital Care's Executive Vice President, E. M. Herndon, reported: "The American Hospital Association has made a flat offer to administer President Kennedy's proposed medical-care-for-the-aged program at the state level through existing Blue Cross Plans, provided the federal government keep its hands off such Blue Cross administration."[5]

The "hands off" sentiment was widespread among most of the major medical, hospital, and insurance institutions, which banded together to create a number of counterproposals. In early 1962, the Hospital Care Association joined forces with 76 other Plans in proposing a new national Blue Cross program for the aged that would be run with assistance from the federal government. But the national Blue Cross and Blue Shield organizations were not able to deliver the promised program by the end of the year and resorted to urging local Plans to develop their own individual efforts to increase enrollment of the aged. The pages of the Hospital Care Association's in-house journal and sales promotional materials from this period highlight numerous "satisfied senior citizen" subscribers and renewed membership drives targeting this now highly sought-after population.

Medical Developments Through the Years
1960

In 1960, the average life expectancy in the United States is 69.7 years. In North Carolina, the numbers are worse for all but white women: 66.9 years for white males, 59.1 for nonwhite males, and 65.3 years old for nonwhite women. White women fare better, expecting to live until age 74.7.

Drugs—their development, use, and abuse—are a hallmark of the 1960s. The number of FDA-approved drugs will grow from about 7,000 in the 1960s to more than 11,700 today.

The oral contraceptive, "the pill," is first approved for use in the United States in 1960 and is credited with revolutionizing sexual behavior and family planning. Within two years, 1.2 million U.S. women are taking the pill.

As the midterm elections approached, Democrats rallied to push the president's health care agenda through. In a dramatic oratorical stand-off, President Kennedy delivered an underwhelming nationally televised speech about his proposal in May 1962, which was followed the next night by a rousing—and highly cautionary—speech from Dr. Edward Annis of the AMA. Dr. Annis characterized the Kennedy program as "a cruel hoax" on the American public, suggesting that they were "in danger of being blitzed, brainwashed, and bandwagoned" into believing that the King-Anderson bill was the only viable medical care program for the elderly.[6] The AMA message triumphed.

Even with the power of President Kennedy's backing, the goal of federally provided health insurance for the elderly remained elusive. Kennedy's legislation found little bipartisan backing, and his other domestic priorities, such as ending racial discrimination, ultimately garnered more of his attention. Furthermore, Republicans had an excellent track record of defeating any kind of health insurance bill that depended on federal administration. One of the most vigorous arguments waged against providing health insurance at no cost—to the elderly or any other group—was based on the idea of "moral hazard." The moral hazard argument asserted that those who are given free services will indulge in riskier behavior and as a result will consume more services than they would if they were paying for them.[7] The vision of a growing class

Did You Know?

President John F. Kennedy's administration had the serious intention of creating a federal program of health insurance for the elderly, which would later be known as Medicare. But when it was first proposed, the program was regarded as a threat to the autonomy of Blue Cross Plans nationwide: the Plans firmly believed they could better support the elderly through voluntary health insurance. Their position was being portrayed negatively by some of the "liberal" media during this period.

The following 1961 private correspondence between the two leaders of North Carolina's prepayment plans, E. M. Herndon of the Hospital Care Association and V. K. Hart of the Hospital Saving Association, reveals their alarm, their resolve, and the pride they held in the services that their respective Associations were providing to the citizens of North Carolina.

On February 6, 1961, V. K. Hart of the Hospital Saving Association wrote: "Voluntary health insurance is facing the fight of its life. Did you hear the 'CBS Reports' on Thursday night of last week? It was an hour-long telecast. Never have I

Health care insurance for the growing senior population became a key concern of the Kennedy administration. In the 1960s, N.C. Blue Plans began offering additional coverage to those needing it most—the elderly, the poor, and students. Photo courtesy of BCBSNC archives.

listened to anything so biased. The medical profession and the Blue Cross Commission were made to look ridiculous. This was all in behalf of care for the aged under Social Security. We, therefore, had better cooperate or else! Our very survival is at stake! We'd better all get in the fight vigorously and fast. The hour is very, very late. Our freedoms are at stake."[3]

On February 20, 1961, E. M. Herndon of the Hospital Care Association responded: "I heard the CBS report you referred to, and I have never heard a more biased, scathing attack against the hospitals, Blue Cross, the medical profession, and voluntary prepayment in general. Those of us in the HCA join you, the Hospital Saving Association, and the N.C. Medical Society in indignation and resentment of this type of thing. We have done what we could to contribute to better health services for all the people of N.C. I know that your interest is entirely unselfish . . . all the health forces in N.C. should join together in full cooperation and understanding in an effort to forestall the government's taking over of the voluntary health programs."[4]

of risk-taking, lazy people devouring expensive health care services at greater expense to the general public was used quite successfully by the opposition.

Hearings on the King-Anderson bill were interrupted by President Kennedy's tragic assassination in November 1963. The best chance for a national health insurance program for the elderly was postponed as the nation was convulsed by the transition in leadership.

Expansion Prompts Cooperation

North Carolina's two Plans increasingly had to conduct their strategic and operational planning with both local and national issues in mind. It was no longer just a matter of competing within the state's borders. Hospital Care and Hospital Saving were also managing national accounts and weathering the recurrent political storms over the prospect of national health insurance. The demographic and economic bases within the state, too, were changing. Although textiles and tobacco were still thriving industries in North Carolina, science and technology companies were beginning to take hold, particularly in the center of the state. In 1959, the nexus of research

1960　　　　　　　　**1961**

Powerful diuretics like Lasix are developed for the treatment of heart failure and edema. Sedatives like Valium are heavily prescribed, and illegal "psychedelic" drugs like LSD find a market among a generation in love with "sex, drugs, and rock 'n' roll."

In 1960, President John F. Kennedy's administration seeks to create a federal program of health insurance for the elderly as part of its domestic agenda. N.C. Blue Plans join others nationwide in supporting voluntary health plans.

The drug thalidomide is revealed to cause severe birth defects and is pulled from markets worldwide in 1961.

universities in the Raleigh–Durham–Chapel Hill area prompted the creation of the Research Triangle Park to attract new industries. By the mid-1960s, the city of Durham was becoming increasingly known for medicine, not tobacco manufacturing alone.

Along with Americans as a whole, most North Carolinians were now seasoned subscribers to some form of health insurance and were demanding coverage that was both cost-effective and comprehensive. Both the Hospital Care and Hospital Saving Associations had been able to meet that demand through alternating periods of intense competition and, at times, necessary cooperation. Certainly the astounding growth they had experienced in their first 30 years continued into the 1960s. In 1962, Hospital Care ceremoniously enrolled its 400,000th member and dedicated its new building at 800 South Duke Street in Durham. Similarly, Hospital Saving's enrollment had surpassed a half million, and its Franklin Street home office building in Chapel Hill was being significantly expanded.

When the Hospital Care Association was accepted into the National Association of Blue Shield Plans in 1962, it prompted a new era of increased cooperation between the two rival Blue Plans in North Carolina. First, Hospital Care began selling the medical service program approved by the state's Medical Society. In addition, the two Associations began to share enrollment of large national and regional accounts. For example, in 1963 the Southern Bell

Telephone and Telegraph Company enrolled more than 70,000 employees in Blue Cross and Blue Shield. Effective management of this large group would require participation from 14 Blue Plans in the Southeast. More than 5,000 employees from the Southern Bell account enrolled in North Carolina, which resulted in the Hospital Care and Hospital Saving Associations agreeing to jointly underwrite the program, with Hospital Care acting as the control plan. This pattern of cooperative underwriting would serve as a precursor to the way the two Associations would interact when faced with the biggest programs they would ever try to administer—Medicare and Medicaid.

President Johnson and Medicare Legislation

In the wake of President Kennedy's death, Lyndon B. Johnson came to office intent on fulfilling and expanding the legacy of his predecessor with regard to race relations, poverty, and health coverage for the elderly.

Almost as soon as he took office, President Johnson sent a special message to Congress advocating the adoption of Medicare through the King-Anderson bill. The proposed legislation was complex in terms of its financing and would require a massive administrative effort. Proponents of the Medicare program needed the expertise of the Blue Plans to understand and plan for all the possible implications. They would also certainly need their established

(facing) George Watts Hill showcases the plan for the Research Triangle Park (RTP). Developed in central North Carolina during the 1960s, RTP attracted new industries—research, technology, and pharmaceutical—that would ultimately change the traditional agricultural base of the state's economy. Photo courtesy of the Research Triangle Foundation.

The Surgeon General first warned that smoking may lead to cancer and other diseases in 1965. The government then mandated that cigarettes carry warning labels about health risks. Photo by Rex Miller, courtesy of the Duke Homestead and Tobacco Museum.

infrastructure to administer it in the event that the legislation passed Congress this time. Blue Cross leaders spent hours testifying before the Ways and Means Committee and conferring with legislators. These consultations provided regular opportunities for them to urge legislators to use the existing private prepayment system instead of replicating it as a potentially unwieldy and costly federal behemoth. Walter J. McNerney, president of the Blue Cross Association, made a compelling case for Blue Cross Plans nationwide to assist the federal government in administering Medicare health benefits and claims processing, declaring, "Blue Cross has the capacity to do a major job for the government. It would fit government into the health care enterprise of the nation instead of vice versa."[8]

Congressional hearings on Medicare and competing proposals came and went through lengthy debates extending from 1963 to 1965. With Johnson's decisive victory over Republican presidential candidate Barry Goldwater in 1964, the balance of power in the House now favored the Democrats. Within the powerful Ways and Means Committee itself, chaired by forceful South Carolina Democrat Wilbur Mills,

the election shifted from 15 Democrats and 10 Republicans to 17 Democrats and 8 Republicans, ensuring a bloc favorable to Medicare. Mills retooled the former King-Anderson bill into Social Security amendments that integrated a compulsory hospitalization program, a voluntary medical insurance program, and expansion of coverage for the medically indigent.

In July 1965, the Social Security amendments passed both houses of Congress and were signed into law by President Johnson. Title XVIII of the Social Security Act established the Medicare program, which would provide health insurance coverage for seniors age 65 or older. Title XIX created the Medicaid program, which combined state and federal medical assistance for the poor. The program was structured as two parts: Part A (hospital insurance), and Part B (medical insurance that covered some physician services, outpatient hospital care, and certain other medical services that Part A did not cover). Neither part would pay for all of a covered person's medical costs, a fact that had helped quell the pervasive Republican concern about "moral hazard." The passage of Medicare and Medicaid ended the bitter, decades-long partisan fight against any form

1961

In 1961, the U.S. Public Health Service begins large-scale use of the Sabin oral vaccine to prevent polio. Drops of the vaccine are placed on sugar cubes that are then fed to children.

Vaccines are one of the greatest achievements of biomedical science and public health in the 20th century. In 1900, only the smallpox vaccine was available for children. By the late 1960s, numerous vaccines have been developed to prevent common infectious diseases. Since these vaccines have become widely available, universally recommended for children, and covered by health insurance, dramatic declines in morbidity rates have occurred.

1962

In 1962, Congress passes the Kefauver-Harris amendments to expand the FDA's control over the expanding pharmaceutical and food industries.

of national health insurance. By this point, Blue Cross leaders had recognized that full cooperation was in their best interest and regarded Medicare as a force for saving the voluntary prepayment system rather than destroying it.[9]

Once Medicare was signed into law, the enormous coordination effort began between the federal government, the voluntary hospital system, and the vast and diverse network of physician providers. As President Johnson described it, the Medicare program would call for "the largest management effort since the Normandy invasion."[10] By using the Blue Plans as intermediaries that would be responsible for reviewing bills from providers and making payments, they would also effectively insulate providers from fear of control by federal bureaucracy. In an interesting concession, Congress gave hospitals the power to nominate their preferred intermediaries for the administration of Medicare Part A. Blue Plans were nominated in 39 states, including North Carolina. An overwhelming majority of the state's hospitals preferred Blue Cross as their intermediary. Both the Hospital Care and Hospital Saving Associations were eager to participate in the Medicare program, and both

also began offering supplemental coverage to subscribers over the age of 65.

It took a year for the details of program administration to be worked out. The first Medicare claim in North Carolina was received by the Hospital Care Association on July 31, 1966—the very first day the Medicare law became effective. A Medicare Administrative Committee, composed of three members of each of the Associations' boards plus staff personnel, was set up and met monthly to discuss Medicare issues. The initial agreement provided for an equal division of claims going to each of the Plans for processing. The Blue Cross national private wire system was expanded to link with the Social Security Administration's Record Center so that queries about eligibility could be answered efficiently. Very quickly, each home office had at least 30 people devoted solely to implementing Medicare. There were also data processing and supervising personnel working part-time to support the Medicare function. In the first six months, more than 31,000 Medicare claims were processed. The overseeing committee soon realized that all Medicare claims should be processed together rather than separately.[11]

1962

Rachel Carson's *Silent Spring* is published in 1962, exposing the hazards of the pesticide DDT for food safety and human health.

1964

In 1964, the U.S. Surgeon General warns that smoking is a major health risk for cancer, cardiovascular disease, and emphysema. By 1965, cigarette package labels are required to read: "Warning: Cigarette Smoking May Be Hazardous to Your Health."

President Lyndon B. Johnson signs the Civil Rights Act in 1964. This sweeping legislation accelerates the trend toward giving African American doctors medical and surgical privileges at formerly whites-only hospitals, where federal funding now depends on having a desegregated staff.

President Lyndon B. Johnson signed legislation creating Medicare and Medicaid in 1965. Rival N.C. Blue Plans finally cooperated to administer the massive new programs. Photo courtesy of BCBSA archives.

Medicare as a Catalyst for Consolidation

The new Medicare program required North Carolina's two historically competitive health insurers to "pull in the same direction in the same harness." The federal government had clearly indicated that having two Plans in North Carolina administer Medicare was awkward. Other external pressures were mounting not only for joint Medicare claims processing but for all other functions as well. Based on its audit findings, the state Department of Insurance was urging cuts in overhead. The national Blue Cross Association wanted the two competing Plans to consolidate but would not intervene. According to Alex McMahon, first president of the consolidated North Carolina Blue Cross and Blue Shield, the BCA position was: "We'll not get involved in local matters because if we do we're likely to bust up the whole system."[12]

The two boards of the Hospital Care and Hospital Saving Associations each selected three members to serve on a joint committee to study the options for and impacts of possible consolidation. The committee concluded that consolidation would be in the best interests of subscribers, providers, hospitals, and the public at large. Its report stated that the recommended consolidation was "not only practicable, but in the light of today's conditions, a necessary step in the interest of good service and efficiency of overall operations."[13] The committee cited the successful experience of the two Plans in working jointly on Medicare and other programs, the increasing need for closer coordination of national accounts, the elimination of duplication of effort, and practical planning for growth and development for the future as specific reasons favoring the move. Many aspects of operations were becoming increasingly computerized, and both Plans were also facing major expenditures in technologies that would nicely facilitate a more compatible infrastructure.

But there were other, less public reasons for consolidation too. Alex McMahon recalled appearing before the joint committee and sharing a hard fact: "We were an embarrassment to the whole Blue Cross and Blue Shield system. I don't know whether they really understood that was the case."[14] He recognized that egos had contributed to keeping the Plans from consolidating when there had long been compelling business reasons for doing so. "They had spent more time competing with one another than they did with the real competition," McMahon noted. The joint committee's recommendation was approved in November 1967, at separate meetings, by the boards of both the Hospital Care and Hospital Saving Associations. North Carolina Blue Cross and Blue Shield, Inc. (NCBCBS)—the

new Plan's first name—was incorporated on January 1, 1968.

After several previous failed attempts to merge Hospital Care and Hospital Saving into one organization, Medicare proved to be the catalyst that finally paved the way for successful consolidation. The procedure had been outlined by the General Statutes under which nonprofit prepayment hospital and medical plans operated in this state. After the move was approved by the subscribers of the respective Plans and the state insurance commissioner, the final step was approval by the new board of trustees, which took place on January 2, 1968. The consolidation made NCBCBS the 14th largest Plan in the United States, covering approximately 25 percent of the state's population, including more than 12,000 employer groups and more than 140,000 subscribers enrolled on a direct-pay basis.

While the state's Blue Plans were finally coming together to better serve the health care needs of its citizens, the nation was in the throes of tremendous political and social upheaval. The Vietnam War had become a quagmire, and public support turned radically against its continuation. Members of the "hippie generation" were making new music and taking new

1965

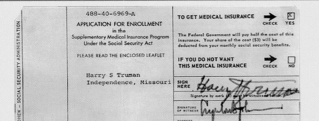

In 1965, Congress passes landmark legislation creating Medicare and Medicaid, greatly expanding access to health care. Blue Cross Plans play a key role in administering the new programs.

In 1965, North Carolina still ranks 43rd in the number of physicians per person.

Now we're better than both of us.

North Carolina Blue Cross & Blue Shield, Inc.

One of us was Hospital Saving Association of Chapel Hill and the other was Hospital Care Association of Durham. Now we're North Carolina Blue Cross and Blue Shield, Inc. And it's better for everyone.

Individuality is good, but when it comes to a good health plan, togetherness is better.

Last year, between the two of us, we served over 25% of the total population of North Carolina. That's a lot of people, but we think you never run out of people to help. And together, we can help more. Like the

other 75%. But besides helping more people, we think we can help them better.

We've both been in business a long time. We have a lot of experience, and because our experiences are different, there's a lot we can do for each other. And more we can do for you.

Just between the two of us, we're glad we waited this long to get together. We're both a little older and a little wiser now. But we just couldn't wait any longer. It was bigger than both of us.

H-7017
This advertisement appears in Magazine — 1968
(200492)

After years of competition, external pressures led to the 1968 consolidation of the Hospital Care and Hospital Saving Associations into one Plan—North Carolina Blue Cross and Blue Shield. Photo courtesy of BCBSNC archives.

drugs—both legal and illegal. Medical care, too, was undergoing dramatic changes. In fact, the decade of the 1960s had seen an explosion of drug development, resulting in hundreds of new patents, including breakthrough medicines such as the oral contraceptive pill and the diuretic Lasix for the treatment of heart failure. Amazing new medical procedures and technologies, including coronary bypass surgery and the first human heart transplant, were yielding

profoundly improved outcomes for cardiac patients. Yet such developments were also driving medical costs skyward. By the end of the decade, Americans were spending more for health care than any other nation in the world.

Given this period of revolutionary change, leadership for North Carolina's new consolidated Blue Plan would be critical. Like health insurers nationwide, the Plan would have to work more efficiently and effectively than ever before to manage rising health care costs so that coverage could remain as affordable and accessible to as many North Carolinians as possible. W. C. Harris, Jr., of Hospital Care was elected the new board president of NCBCBS. Neither of the former longtime presidents of the respective organizations—E. M. Herndon of the Hospital Care Association and E. B. Crawford of the Hospital Saving Association—would be selected for the helm of the new organization; instead, they would serve as senior vice presidents. In all of the previous consolidation efforts, each had maintained that any new board should have equal representation from each Association so that the balance of power would not be tipped unfairly toward one Plan or the other. The new combined board of NCBCBS would retain that balance and have equal representation and be composed of 24 trustees from the general public, the hospitals, and physicians.

But there could only be one president of the new North Carolina Blue Cross and Blue Shield. Would that person be from Hospital Care or

Hospital Saving? In the end, John Alexander (Alex) McMahon was named as the new president. McMahon had been serving as vice president of Special Development for Hospital Saving since 1965 and had proven a savvy negotiator who seemed to have the best business interests of the Associations in mind during the consolidation effort. It is a little-known fact that McMahon had, in fact, told the board of Hospital Saving that he would resign if the Plan did not agree to join with Hospital Care. In McMahon's judgment, the stubborn refusal to consolidate "was just plain dumb."[15] McMahon stayed, and the Associations gave in to the merger plan—for reasons both practical and political.

"We Were One"

The task of bringing together two organizations that had been in competition for over 30 years would be formidable. Bill Houck, who had been with Hospital Saving since its founding in a number of roles, described the challenge: "The two Plans had operated separately for so long that very important differences had developed in the way they operated and even in their philosophies."[16] Both had expanded their staffs, so there were many people in duplicate roles competing for positions of authority in the new organization. But McMahon's approach to integrating the two organizations was unwavering: "I made it clear that I was going to brook no old rivalries, and I was going to choose the best person for whatever the job was."[17] He also quickly allayed fears about possible layoffs by announcing that all of the more than 850 employees would be retained, at least during the early transition period.

Further, there were six buildings being used as home offices and dozens of district offices statewide to consolidate in some way. Although Hospital Care had bought additional property for expansion on Morehead Avenue in Durham in late 1967 and Hospital Saving had also bought an additional tract on the Chapel Hill–Durham Boulevard, the initial plan was to continue operations out of the existing home offices previously occupied by Hospital Care and Hospital Saving. But even before the consolidation had been formalized, Alex McMahon had anticipated the need for a new—and symbolically neutral—executive office that had never been occupied by either Hospital Care or Hospital Saving. McMahon recalled: "I knew it wouldn't make any sense to go back and forth between Durham and Chapel Hill and have an office in both places. So I bought some property in the name of Blue Cross and Blue Shield out on the boulevard where the building is today. There was a farmhouse on the acreage, and I put my office in the farmhouse to establish the principle that we were one. We were not Durham, we were not Chapel Hill. We were North Carolina Blue Cross and Blue Shield."[18]

Within the first six months after consolidation, the new corporation was reorganized

Prescription drug development exploded in the 1960s, growing from 7,000 FDA-approved medications to nearly 12,000 today. Illegal drug use also escalated during the era of "sex, drugs, and rock 'n' roll." Photo courtesy of BCBSNC archives.

After more than 30 years of service, longtime leaders E. B. Crawford of Hospital Saving (left) and E. M. Herndon of Hospital Care (right) retired in 1968. J. Alexander (Alex) McMahon (far right) was named as the first president of the consolidated Plan. Photo courtesy of BCBSNC archives.

into eight divisions: Administration, Finance, Planning, Claims, Sales, Blue Shield Activities, Provider Relations, and Public Relations. With a new structure established, the most pressing business need was to integrate the various kinds of coverage that existed in the two Plans and emerge with a new product. By the end of 1968, NCBCBS was ready to unveil its new certificate, which represented a broader, more flexible approach to health care. The goal of this certificate was to reduce high-cost inpatient medical care by increasing:

- testing prior to hospital admission
- outpatient treatment and diagnostic benefits
- post-hospital care in less expensive extended care facilities
- use of hospital progressive or minimal care units.[19]

By the end of its first year, NCBCBS had a net increase in membership of 54,820. That year, 1968, also proved to be a banner year for Blue Plans nationwide, which experienced the greatest increase in enrollment in nine years; Blue Plans now covered more than 40 percent of the U.S. population.

1966

Research published in 1966 demonstrates that screening mammograms save women's lives.

1967

In 1967, the World Health Organization undertakes a global program to eradicate smallpox, which still threatens 60 percent of the world's population, killing every fourth victim and eluding any form of treatment.

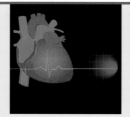

Cardiovascular disease remains the leading cause of death in the United States. But amazing new heart procedures and technologies are making news, as coronary bypass surgery and the first human heart transplant are performed in 1967.

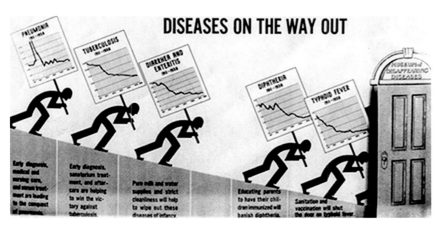

Vaccine-Preventable Disease	Year Vaccine Developed or Licensed	Decrease in morbidity
Diptheria	1923	100%
Pertussis	1926	95.7%
Tetanus	1927	97.4%
Poliomyelitis	1955	100%
Measles	1963	100%
Mumps	1966	99.6%
Rubella	1969	99.3%

By the late 1960s, vaccines had been developed to prevent many of the common infectious diseases that had been among the leading causes of death for decades. Photo courtesy of the University of Pennsylvania.

Routine childhood immunization contributed to dramatic declines in morbidity and mortality. Photo courtesy of Duke University Medical Archives.

New Blue—New Building

As 1969 opened, the "NewBlue" certificate was being widely promoted, and coverage previously issued by Hospital Care and Hospital Saving converted to it. Advertisements from this period reveal the new branding of the product—a distinctly contemporary look and messaging that continued for decades. The change that was represented in NewBlue coverage was not simply a reflection of a new corporate identity. It also represented a fundamental shift in the underlying concept of prepayment from sickness coverage to health coverage, so that benefits included the "vertical" as well as the "horizontal" patient. A new program of dental benefits was also initiated. In another significant business development, NCBCBS learned that it would begin acting as an intermediary for the federal government's new Title IX Medicaid program as of January 1, 1970. The company also took steps to assume a more meaningful role in regional and state health planning, as Alex McMahon was appointed by Governor Dan K. Moore to develop a new, comprehensive health planning program for the state.

Human resource policies and practices of the new North Carolina Blue Cross and Blue Shield in some ways began to reflect an increasing concern for diversity and respectful relations in the workplace. For example, the company adopted the Affirmative Action program on January 1, 1968—the first day the consolidation became effective. As a result, the percentage of minority employees at NCBCBS grew from 2.6 to 9.5 percent between 1968 and 1969. Yet articles such as "What Women Should Know about Football" and "Keypunch Goes Indian" in the Plan's in-house publications still disclose a lack of awareness about the prescriptive gender roles and lingering racial biases of the times.[20]

As the decade closed, on December 30, 1969, a big announcement hit the newspapers. North Carolina Blue Cross and Blue Shield unveiled its plans to construct a new $5 million home office building to serve as the corporate headquarters. The site for the building would be a 39-acre tract on the Chapel Hill–Durham Boulevard within sight of the farmhouse office where McMahon and a small staff had been working since the consolidation. It would ultimately replace four of the six buildings that were being used as the home office complex. However, until construction was completed, the six offices would be fully used and additional space might even be used for interim growth. The South Duke Street building would be used as a government operations center for administration of Medicare, Medicaid, federal employee, and CHAMPUS programs. The West Franklin Street building in Chapel Hill and the Geer Street building in Durham would be sold.

The Plan signed a contract for architectural services with A. C. Odell, Jr., and Associates of Charlotte, who would need approximately a year to complete the plans. The Nello Teer Company of Durham was selected as the general contractor for the project, and construction was scheduled to begin in January 1971. Depending upon the final design, it would take approximately two years to complete construction. NCBCBS made clear in its press releases that all of the funding for the new building would come from its reserves in order to alleviate any subscriber concerns about possible rate increases.

There were many advantages to using the Plan's new building as its headquarters and the Duke Street building for government operations:

- The land available at both tracts met current needs and was expected to allow for 10 to 15 years of future growth.
- Both sites were already owned by NCBCBS.
- The two sites would afford maximum flexibility to meet changing programs in the future.
- Present operations could continue without interruption during construction of the new building.
- Staff travel time between the current six locations would be greatly reduced.
- The site would afford maximum convenience for employee parking.

- The need to transfer clerical staff between Durham and Chapel Hill would be virtually eliminated.
- The corporation would have excellent access to both the Chapel Hill and Durham labor markets.[21]

At the close of the 1960s, growth of the now-consolidated North Carolina Blue Cross and Blue Shield was anticipated to continue exponentially for the foreseeable future, as it had for its predecessor Plans, the Hospital Care and Hospital Saving Associations. Health care costs were also expected to double or triple in the next decade, with prepayment plans and government programs assuming an increasing part of the costs. The Plan would need to develop new cost containment initiatives such as utilization review and hospital cost educational programs to try to maintain its financial health. A multi-million-dollar building was under construction. Electronic data processing was expanded to provide a management information system for storage and retrieval of the millions of data files and required three shifts of employees around the clock to staff it.

1968

1969

North Carolina Blue Cross & Blue Shield, Inc.

In 1968, after 35 years of competition, the Hospital Care and Hospital Saving Associations consolidate to become North Carolina Blue Cross and Blue Shield in order to better serve the health care needs of the state's citizens.

Americans pay more for medical care than any other people—$60.3 billion in 1969, nearly 500 percent more than they spent in 1950. U.S. doctors' fees are rising twice as fast as consumer prices; hospital costs are soaring five times faster.

The era of "New Blue" in North Carolina was decidedly under way. After years of parallel development and head-to-head competition, the state's founding prepayment health insurance Plans had consolidated into a vibrant new corporation that was among the largest Blue Plans in the nation. The longtime leaders of the two parent Plans, E. M. Herndon and E. B. Crawford, retired in 1968, and new leadership was in place under Alex McMahon. Federal Medicare legislation had proven to be the final catalyst needed to bring the Hospital Care and Hospital Saving Associations together. However, the battle over a federal health insurance program did not end with the passage of Medicare and Medicaid. The battle merely shifted to an ongoing debate about what the appropriate level of funding for such programs should be. The origins of Medicare during the 1960s would also shape the dispute over national health insurance in the 1970s, an era during which health policy would continue to draw strong reactions from the Congress and the public.

While an explosion of medical technology and pharmaceutical development had begun providing new treatments and hope for many, it also fueled an unrelentingly upward spiral in health care costs. The "new" NCBCBS would need careful planning and innovative programs to manage these runaway costs and continue its mission of serving the health care needs of all North Carolinians. The social and political unrest of the 1960s would soon give way to the economic upheavals of the 1970s, in which the financing and delivery of health care would take a radical turn.

(facing) While cardiovascular disease has remained the leading cause of death for decades, advances in medical technology during the 1960s began to yield new hope through treatments such as coronary bypass surgery (shown) and the miracle of human heart transplants. Photo courtesy of the National Institutes of Health.

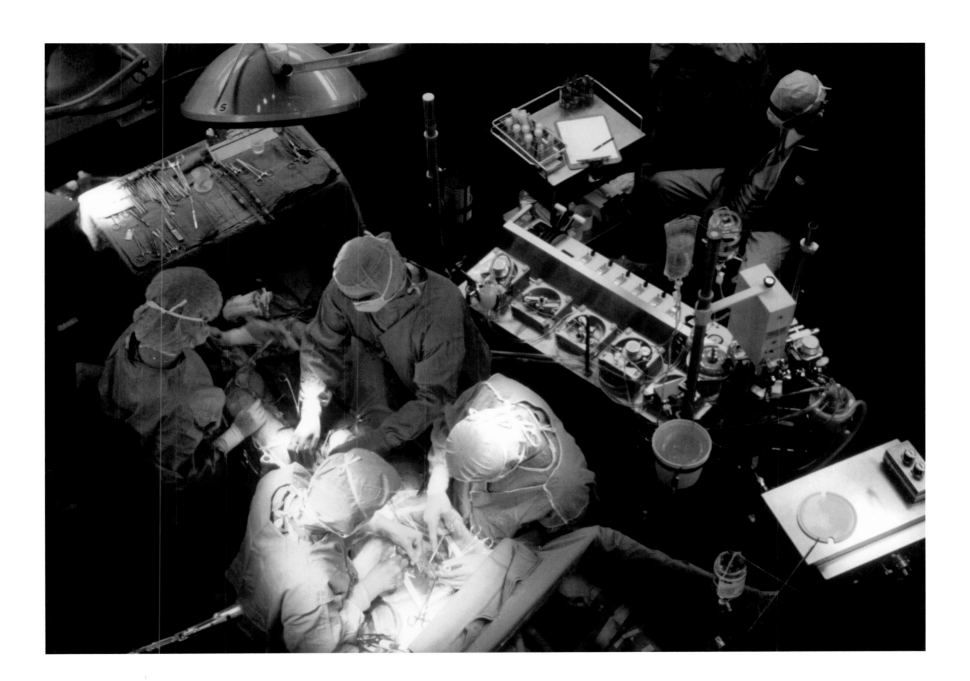

Chapter Five

New Blue, Now a Big Business

The Rise of Managed Care

As the newly consolidated North Carolina Blue Cross and Blue Shield entered the 1970s, it faced the significant internal challenges of forging a new Plan identity and merging operations. But external pressures were mounting, too. Health care costs were skyrocketing as never before. The rate of inflation of hospital costs had climbed from 6.9 percent in 1960 to 14.8 percent in 1970. New technologies such as CAT scans and expensive procedures including open heart surgery required doctors to have more assistants available to help perform them. Physicians raised their "customary" fees, and nursing salaries were up 100 percent over the previous decade. NCBCBS would face significant economic hurdles in its efforts to bring affordable health insurance to the state's growing and diverse population.

Not only were costs rising at an alarming rate, but there had also been a dramatic increase in the utilization of health care by both the aged and poor since the passage of Medicare and Medicaid legislation in 1965. While the public appreciated the social value of these entitlement programs, predicted expenditures for administering them had been grossly underestimated—by more than $1 billion. Although President Lyndon B. Johnson had successfully ushered in these entitlement programs at the peak of the civil rights movement, the Vietnam War prepared the way for his political demise and a Republican victory in the 1968 presidential election. Once Richard Nixon was in office, he began to hear the widespread clamor for health care reform aimed at containing runaway costs. In response to this pressure, President Nixon declared a health care "crisis" in 1969, stating, "Unless action is taken within the

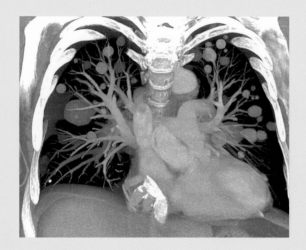

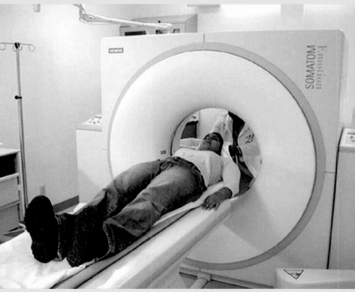

Medical imaging technologies developed in the 1970s, such as the CAT scan, provided remarkable new views of the body. While imaging offers valuable and detailed diagnostic information, it continues to be costly to perform and contributes to high treatment costs for patients. Photos courtesy of the National Institutes of Health and the Internet Stroke Center.

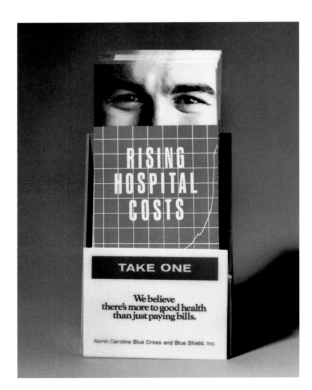

Hospital costs doubled between 1960 and 1970. NCBCBS attempted to help members understand the changing health care environment and intensified its cost-containment efforts through utilization review. Photo courtesy of BCBSNC archives.

next two or three years . . . we will have a massive breakdown in our medical system."[1] In an attempt to address these concerns, the president ordered price controls in health care and other economic sectors and appointed America's first "czar" to enforce them. His administration also hoped to craft a market reform strategy that would bring costs under control without moving the country in the direction of national health insurance.

The Nixon administration quickly found its strategy through the leadership of Dr. Paul Ellwood, a Minnesota neurologist. Ellwood reflected the fears of many traditional practitioners in believing that Medicare might be an opening wedge toward socialized medicine; he also believed that fee-for-service plans penalized physicians and medical institutions that returned patients to "healthy" status. He proposed a new delivery model that would be a better alternative to a state-controlled system, provide quality service to the public, and also contain escalating health care costs by preventing disease and maintaining good health in the population. Ellwood called this model the Health Maintenance Organization (HMO). The HMO would compete on the basis of price and quality,

combining insurance and health care into a single organization.[2] In May 1970, Ellwood met with administration officials from the Department of Health, Education, and Welfare, who then adopted his HMO model as the centerpiece of the Nixon administration's health care strategy. In 1971, the president unveiled his plan to cut health care costs and to spur development of health maintenance organizations as a better way to provide care for Medicare and Medicaid recipients. It would be the first move in the radical transformation of health care delivery from traditional fee-for-service plans to what would come to be known as "managed care."

The Transitional Years (1968–1973)

During its first two years as a new company, NCBCBS was subject to the same seismic shifts in the health care landscape that were occurring at the national level. But the company may not have felt these changes as keenly, because it was preoccupied with restructuring personnel, streamlining operations, coordinating information technology systems, and planning for the new headquarters building. As Alex McMahon, president of NCBCBS at that time, readily

In 1970, the average life expectancy in the United States is 70.8 years. In North Carolina, the numbers remain lower: 66.8 years for white males, and only 58.8 for nonwhite males. White women are the exception, living until age 75.7, but nonwhite women are only expected to live 67.8 years.

The era of "managed care" begins in 1970, when the Nixon administration adopts the Health Maintenance Organization (HMO) as a new model for delivering and financing health care.

acknowledged, "The concerns were internal, about bringing these two organizations together."[3] The company had to learn how one organization does the work of two, and that learning curve naturally precipitated many problems—both expected and unexpected. Implementing the conversion to a new certificate of coverage was a huge undertaking, and preparations to serve as a fiscal agent for the new Title XIX Medicaid program at the beginning of 1970 was yet another major demand on the new NCBCBS.

Despite the significant challenges inherent in the consolidation effort, there was measurable progress. NCBCBS began expanding its portfolio by introducing an innovative new program of dental coverage in 1969. The government programs—Medicare, Medicaid, and CHAMPUS—drove growth and accounted for more than 50 percent of the Plan's total business volume in 1970. Heritage companies across the state were choosing the "new" Blue Plan for their employees because of its ability to offer affordable rates for coverage of large and small groups alike. The tobacco giant, R. J. Reynolds Corporation, increased its group enrollment to 40,000 employees in 1970, making it the largest employer account to date. The company also became the first Plan in the country to offer an ambulatory or outpatient surgery program as a cost containment measure—an innovation rolled out in 1971 in cooperation with the former Watts Hospital in Durham. Construction of the new headquarters building also began in 1971 and,

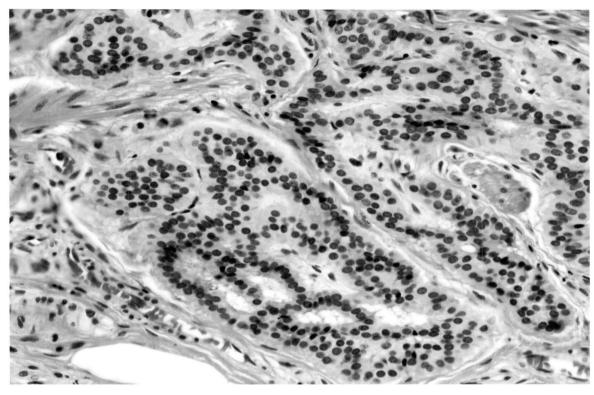

Colon cancer cells. The rising incidence of cancer in the United States led President Nixon to declare "war" on cancer in 1971 and call for increased funding for research. Photo courtesy of the Cancer Media Centre.

with it, the promise of increased efficiency and the literal blending of the temporarily scattered staffs. In 1972, the Plan won the state contract to administer the health insurance program for North Carolina state employees, which required rapid, massive preparation in order to develop all the related manuals and forms for the 330 employing units across the state. "We were faced with enrolling 150,000 subscribers in a matter of five weeks," recalled Pete Dorer, billing director for NCBCBS at the time.[4]

In some ways, growth itself was fueling a concerning financial trend. The substantial increase in business volume also required the hiring of more employees, and more employees required the Plan to rent two more temporary office spaces until the new building could be completed. In fact, the NCBCBS workforce reached a high of 1,000 employees in 1972. The unexpected levels of claims processing driven by the government programs necessitated more sophisticated computer automation and more skilled employees. But the biggest drain on the company's resources was the same as for every other Blue Cross and Blue Shield Plan in the nation—exponential increases in health care costs. So despite the largest annual enrollment increase in the organization's history,

NCBCBS suffered a $6 million operating loss in 1971, continuing a disturbing trend the company had been experiencing since the consolidation. With steely resolve, Alex McMahon declared in his 1971 president's report, "We must and will find a solution to the loss problem that has plagued us for the past three years."[5]

But McMahon would not be the Plan president who would have to face these financial woes. In 1972, he accepted a position as the president of the American Hospital Association, and Rogers C. Wade stepped in as acting president while the board sought new leadership. Through his activities with the national Blue Cross and Blue Shield Association, McMahon had a broad acquaintance with many other Plan leaders and had admired a very capable potential candidate named Thomas A. (Tom) Rose, then vice president of the Cleveland Plan. McMahon suggested that the board interview him, and in 1973 Rose was named the new NCBCBS president.

As Rose began his new role, he was inheriting many of the top people from the two antecedent organizations, now trying to work together. But he quickly recognized that many of these people had not gotten over the competitive atmosphere that existed previously. Rose recalled: "One

1970

1971

Legislation that would establish the first single health insurance program to cover all Americans is introduced by Senator Edward Kennedy in 1970, but it never passes.

Research published in 1970 establishes amniocentesis as a source of critical information about genetic abnormalities such as Down syndrome.

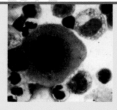

President Richard Nixon declares "war on cancer" in 1971. Chemotherapy soon joins the ranks of routine treatments, especially for breast cancer.

In the early 1970s, research on neurotransmitters demonstrates that mental states are the result of complicated physiology and brain chemistry, giving rise to the development of highly effective new antidepressants.

long-term employee told me, 'There are ten individual organizations operating under the umbrella of Blue Cross and Blue Shield of North Carolina, and your first job is going to be to pull all that together and make it run as one cohesive organization.' And I found that was very, very true—that the merger had only taken place in name and had not been fully implemented. This dichotomy was not just at the operating level but it existed at the board of trustees level too."[6]

When Rose arrived, the NCBCBS board was composed of 24 people: eight physicians, eight hospital administrators, and eight members from the public at large with no health care affiliations. Physicians and hospital administrators had traditionally been appointed by the N.C. Hospital Association and the N.C. Medical Society—a vestige of the "old way" of doing business at the Plan. This practice was common not only in North Carolina but in Plans across the nation, and was increasingly subject to significant challenge from the public and political leaders alike. Critics skeptical of the long-standing close relationship between hospitals and Blue Plans were concerned that there was a conflict of interest that worked against the customer. The public needed reassurance that reimbursement mechanisms were being fairly negotiated and administered and were not contributing to rate increases.[7]

To stem this growing concern, directors of the national Blue Cross Association (BCA) passed a resolution in 1971 calling for majority public

A Sign of the Times

Bill Pully, president of the North Carolina Hospital Association, acknowledged that rising health care costs drive the problems that most hospitals have, resulting in growing tensions and rigorous contract negotiations with payers such as the government and the whole range of insurers, including BCBSNC: "Historically, the hospitals had been well represented on the Blue Cross and Blue Shield of North Carolina board. There had been a collaborative relationship between the insurer and the hospitals of North Carolina, which were given preferential pricing. In many ways, BCBSNC helped hospitals do a better job, and we've often thought that they knew more about our hospitals than we did because they were so intimately involved for so many years with their operation. That changed over 20 years ago because the environment changed for both health insurance companies and for hospitals, and it became necessary to eliminate that very close relationship.

"Now how you feel about Blue Cross and Blue Shield of North Carolina or any payer on any given date may depend on how the last contract negotiation went. But I think we all recognize that BCBSNC and other payers have a role to play in the health care delivery system, as do hospitals, and sometimes those roles appear at cross purposes. Other times they're a little more aligned. We have very good channels of communication, and we meet regularly with each other. Representatives of BCBSNC attend all of our membership meetings. So we really reach out to find ways to work together."[9]

representation on all Plan boards. NCBCBS changed its former practice and moved into compliance by allowing only those board nominations made by a committee of private citizens who had no ties to any health care organizations. But political pressure continued to mount, leading to a complete separation of the American Hospital Association (AHA) and the Blue Cross Association. In 1973, the AHA insignia that had originally been the center of the Blue Cross symbol was replaced with a stylized human figure reminiscent of a famous Leonardo da Vinci drawing, symbolizing humanity. This historic

In 1973, the seal of the American Hospital Association was removed from the Blue Cross symbol and replaced by the silhouette of a stylized human figure in a circle, symbolizing humanity. The Blue Cross and Blue Shield symbols have gone through subtle changes over the years, but the strength of the Blue Brands has remained constant. Photo courtesy of BCBSA.

change—in the relationship between AHA and BCA, as well as the symbol itself—was evident in the marked tensions between hospitals and Blue Plans everywhere and reflected both the escalating demand for and resulting strain of cost control efforts (see *A Sign of the Times*).[8]

A New Era in a New Building

The year 1973 proved to be a watershed for NCBCBS in many ways. On May 1, Tom Rose began what would be a 20-year tenure as president of the company. After several years of planning and construction, the innovatively designed new corporate headquarters, known as the Service Center, opened in July and was dedicated in October of that year (see *The Building* inset).

Soon after the Hospital Care and Hospital Saving Associations consolidated to form North Carolina Blue Cross and Blue Shield (NCBCBS) in 1968, plans for a new home office building were launched. Since its dedication in 1973, the building—with its distinctive shape and reflective design—has become an iconic part of the Research Triangle area landscape. Decades later, it remains a local landmark, a subject of architectural interest and perpetual curiosity, and an ongoing symbol of North Carolina's greatest health insurance success story.

To follow the building from conceptualization to construction, from Service Center to Corporate Headquarters, is to follow the company's history of growth and expansion.

The Site

When two long-standing competitors merge, the issue of where the new company will "live" has more than just operational significance. The deci-sion often indicates whether power will truly be shared or whether one of the former competitors will be more dominant. It can build confidence in the newly integrated staff or breed fear of layoffs. It can contribute to the creation of a new organizational culture or signal an impending fracture. The importance of this decision was not lost on Alex McMahon, the first president of the newly consolidated North Carolina Blue Cross and Blue Shield.

Under the guidance of Rogers C. Wade, senior vice president acting as the coordinator for the building program, NCBCBS began exploring location possibilities. It studied sites in the Research Triangle Park, downtown Durham, and some suburban areas. But there was another option. Prior to consolidation, the Hospital Saving Association had bought some acreage on the Durham–Orange County line, with front-age on U.S. Highway 15-501, also known as the Durham–Chapel Hill Boulevard. Route 15-501 is the primary corridor between Chapel Hill and

An early architectural model reveals a building plan with a traditional rectangular structure. The final rhomboid design employed solar design principles well before "going green" was in vogue. Photo courtesy of BCBSNC archives.

Durham, so from a practical perspective, a location along this boulevard seemed ideal.

But it was also a metaphor of the middle ground, a neutral site where the former Chapel Hill-based Hospital Saving and Durham-based Hospital Care Associations could come together after years of territorial competition and physical separation of their several office buildings. Soon the company purchased additional acreage from a local farmer, resulting in a 39-acre tract on 15-501 as the site for a centralized office building that would bring together many of the staff members of its two parent Plans. President McMahon's decision to place his executive office in the farmhouse on this property while the new building was under construction was intentionally symbolic. And his resolve to create unity was unequivocal: "We were not Durham, we were not Chapel Hill. We were North Carolina Blue Cross and Blue Shield."[1]

The Design

George Watts Hill, the Durham businessman who helped launch the Hospital Care Association in 1933, had strongly influenced the successful consolidation of the state's competing Blue Cross and Blue Shield Plans. The merger provided him an opportunity to collaborate with renowned architect A. G. "Goulie" Odell on a creative design for the Plan's new home.[2] NCBCBS quickly signed a contract with Odell Associates, Inc., of Charlotte for complete architectural services, including interior design and landscaping. The building would need to accommodate from 5 to 20 years' worth of employee growth, but its style was initially undetermined. As Wade stated early in the planning process, "Whether it will be a large high-rise building, a central building with a number of surrounding buildings for various operations, or a cluster of buildings of various sizes has not been worked out."[3] In early 1970, the architects made several topographic and other studies of the site and proposed their first design. Plan President McMahon was astonished: "The first drawings Odell showed me were absolutely out to lunch. They looked like fortresses with parapets and all that kind of stuff. And I said, 'Back to the drawing board!' Then they came up with that rhomboid."[4]

Just how did they come up with the seeds of what would one day be an award-winning design? George Watts Hill recalled, "Goulie and myself got to laughing about it, and I said, 'Just lay the damn building down.' We just laid it down. Then it was Goulie's idea to have it so that the sun didn't hit it but just the absolute minimum."[5] The rhomboid—a three-dimensional parallelogram—was not only an innovative and highly contemporary shape, but also one that had many inherent economies based on passive solar design principles. The exterior walls of the building would be glass and would slope 45 degrees to the south and west, minimizing direct solar radiation in the summer and reducing air conditioning needs, yet maximizing that radia-

tion in the winter and conserving heat. "The sun's rays will only strike the glass at acute angles, thus reducing glare and heat gain," explained E. H. Copeland, Jr., of Odell Associates.[6] The reflective glass would also make the facade of the building an ever-changing mirror of the surrounding natural environment. The goal was to have the building blend into the existing pastoral landscape, both to enhance the site and to shield it from excessive highway noise.

The new home office would be 90 feet wide and 500 feet long, with five stories—four at and above ground level and one below. The angled slope of the walls would allow about 80 percent of the 225,000 square feet of floor space to be useable for work areas, most of which would be column free. It was believed that from the time the building would first be occupied in 1973, this seemingly ample space would easily meet the Plan's expected growth over the coming 10 to 15 years, housing up to 1,000 employees. The 39-acre site was also large enough for another building of similar size to be built if the original building became inadequate. In fact, the original architectural plan included three additional construc-

The land facing Highway 15-501 was sold to NCBCBS because the owner could not figure out how to get his cattle across the increasingly busy road. Site preparation began in the fall of 1970. Photo courtesy of BCBSNC archives.

tion phases of 100,000 square feet each, revealing the Plan's recognition that growth might not be merely steady, but could be unprecedented by the end of the twentieth century.[7]

The entrance area to the giant rhomboid would be a 200-foot reflecting pool with a fountain, surrounded by a circular drive, providing easy access to the building. In the center of the pool would be a massive steel sculpture to be designed by public artists William Severson and Saunders Shultz of the Scopia Company, based

Construction began in January 1971 and took more than two years to complete. Photo courtesy of BCBSNC archives.

in St. Louis, Missouri. They were charged with creating a clear visual identity for the new headquarters building, and they began interviewing staff members and the architects for background and ideas.[8]

When plans for the building were first announced, the late 1969 cost estimate for construction was $5 million. But by September 1970 the number cited in the press had climbed to $7 million, and ultimately the total would reach almost $10 million. Throughout the design and construction phases, NCBCBS was careful to communicate that all building costs were coming from the sale of 9 of its 11 current offices and established reserve funds, not from rate increases to its members, in an effort to maintain public support for its expansion.

The Construction and Move

The first step in moving from the design to the construction phase was petitioning for a special use building permit from the Town of Chapel Hill. Once the permit was approved in September 1970, site preparation began. Initial projections were for completion by the mid-1970s, but due to the company's explosive growth during the first two years following consolidation, the construction timetable was advanced in hopes of occupying the building sometime in 1973. By January 1971, construction was under way.

The challenging assignment of building the high-profile, contemporary rhomboid structure

fell to the Nello Teer Company of Durham. Nello Teer's construction field supervisor, Bruce Bland, acknowledged, "The building looks complicated, but in some ways it was just a regular job. The toughest thing was starting in the wintertime. It was so cold that when you sat down on that structural steel it would stick to your pants. And sometimes the mud underneath that first floor was up to our knees."[9] Bland also remembered that board member and Plan founder George Watts Hill came by every day over the two-year construction period to talk with the crew, answer questions, and share his excitement about their progress. Plan president Alex McMahon and his staff had a unique vantage point on the developing construction from the old farmhouse on the property where the executive offices were originally located. Betsy Parker, Plan employee since 1972, recalled being told by one of the executive staff members, "From the window where they worked they could see the building as it went up. That was an amazing feat for them, because day after day they saw the earth being moved and the girders being put up."[10] But eventually the farmhouse had to be torn down to make way for new construction.

By April 1973, the nearly 5,000 panes of reflective glass were being installed. As the time to move into the building approached, both anxiety and curiosity were apparent in the questions that employees were asking about the structure of their new home: "Can we get fresh air ventilation if the air conditioning fails?"

The angled placement of almost 5,000 panes of reflective glass minimizes direct solar radiation in the summer and reduces air-conditioning needs. In winter, they help capture and conserve heat. Photos courtesy of BCBSNC archives.

Rhomboid: a three-dimensional parallelogram

Key statistics:
- 90 feet wide
- 500 feet long
- 5 stories—4 at or above ground level, 1 below
- 45 degree slope of the exterior walls
- 225,000 square feet

An urban legend: Perhaps because of its unusual shape, a persistent and widespread rumor exists that the building was constructed "backwards"—that the upward slope was meant to face southward rather than northward, as it does. Both the architectural firm and construction company that developed this building confirm that the rumor is merely that: an interesting but untrue speculation.

"Has the building been tested to see if birds are going to fly into it?" "Will any adverse wind conditions be created by the building's shape?"[11] But as in all major transitions, there was also poignancy about leaving the "Old Blue" behind. As Betsy Parker, now director of Network Management Operations and Support for Blue Cross and Blue Shield of North Carolina, explained, "We were all excited about the move because the building was going to be beautiful, it was going to be state of the art, we'd even have a cafeteria! But then there was a little bit of sadness to leave the downtown area of Chapel Hill where we were all so accustomed to eating out and had been for so long."[12]

Finally, over four consecutive weekends in July 1973, Neptune Moving transported the office furniture, equipment, boxes of files, and computers to the new headquarters site. One by one, the various work areas on each floor were set up and readied for occupancy by the more than 800 employees who would settle in by the end of the month. Despite the excitement about moving in, there were a few initial snafus. A minor plumbing problem prevented the food services crew from serving hot meals the first few days, but they rallied and provided pimento cheese sandwiches until the cafeteria could operate as planned.[13]

After a few months of settling in, the building was formally dedicated on a crisp autumn day—October 19, 1973—in a gala celebration attended by employees, Board members, the public, and the press. George Watts Hill, who had

Beauty among the beams. Because of its rhomboid design and sleek aesthetic, the building was featured in the New York Times Magazine, Newsweek, *design exhibits at New York's Museum of Modern Art, and a Toyota advertisement.*

(facing) The construction supervisor recalled the working conditions in winter: "It was so cold that when you sat down on that structural steel it would stick to your pants. And sometimes the mud underneath that first floor was up to our knees." Photos courtesy of BCBSNC archives.

A big job for window washers.

The angled walls posed some interesting challenges in the planning and installation of interior work spaces. Photos courtesy of BCBSNC archives.

shepherded the building design and construction ever since the tract of land had been purchased, proudly proclaimed "Mission Accomplished" in his remarks at the dedication ceremony.[14] BCBSNC headquarters was now known as the "Service Center" in an effort to emphasize the Plan's commitment to service. "New Blue" had its new home.

The Sculptures

In keeping with the startling slant and modern rhomboid design, several sculptures were created to punctuate the building grounds and interiors. The most pronounced of these is the commanding steel sculpture rising out of the pool at the main entrance. Scopia's core idea for the final design came from the artists' study of the company's culture and working environment, and the growing importance of computer technology to its operations. Because it mimics the shape of a computer chip, they named the sculpture *Computer Connectors*.[15] At 48 feet tall and 42,000 pounds, painted in the company's signature blue, the sculpture invited visitors to make their own meaning of its three-part shape. In the years since its completion in 1973, the sculpture became known as the "Triune Towers" and has been described as depicting three hands that symbolize the working relationship among the subscribers, health care providers, and the Plan.

The plaza at the ground-level entrance to the

building was also flanked by sculptures at its east and west ends. Ranging from 11 to 21 feet tall, the sculptures reflected the outlines of the Blue Cross and Blue Shield symbols onto the building glass above. Like the rhomboid itself, each sculpture was cut at 45 degree angles and is constructed from metallic pipes originally designed to vibrate from the rhythm of the wind. When there was insufficient wind to create the desired musical sound, the next plan was to place a machine below ground to generate the needed level of vibration. But as Building Complex Manager Gerald White revealed, "The engineers finally figured out that it would just vibrate the concrete apart, so they never did use it."[16]

Inside the lobby on the ground floor, mounted on the opposing walls, there were two "maze" sculptures also designed by Scopia. They represented BCBSNC's leadership role in charting a course through the complexity of modern medical care. The maze sculptures were replaced in 2002 with a large abstract painting and an elegant wood wall displaying the company name.

The Public Response

Ever since the Service Center opened its doors in 1973, and despite the company sign at the entrance, there has been ongoing—and often amusing—speculation by passersby about this uniquely shaped building. Travelers on the Chapel Hill–Durham Boulevard have often pulled in to what they thought was a rest area.

Employees began working in this unusual environment in July 1973. Photo courtesy of BCBSNC archives.

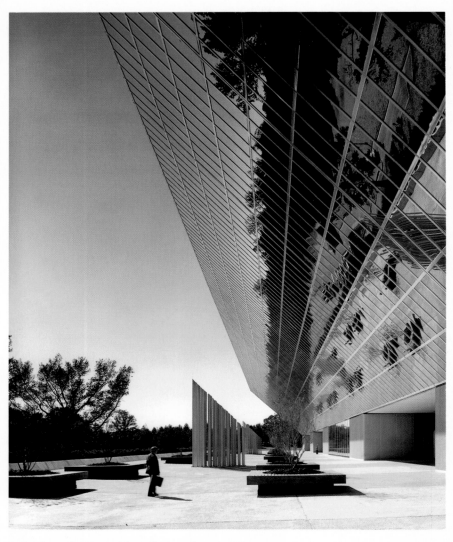

View from the plaza. The reflective glass mirrors the shield and cross sculptures, as well as the surrounding natural environment. Photo courtesy of BCBSNC archives.

Others have thought it was a sports stadium. One person even thought the roof of the building was a landing strip! The original reflecting pool in front also lured in people seeking to cool off from the summer heat. Former switchboard operator Doris Black recalled two elderly ladies who entered the lobby and asked, "Are there really people upstairs?"[17]

In fact, the Plan inaugurated a home office guided tour program as early as 1969 to help people understand what the company had to offer, attract new employees, and orient new staff. With the advent of the new Service Center, the tour program took on a whole new energy and was offered on a reservation-only basis. Each Thursday, uniformed "girl guides" used detailed scripts to lead visitors through the various areas of the building. The hour-long tours offered information about the company's history, facts about the Service Center's architectural features, and an introduction to each major operational area.[18] As times changed, so did the need for the guides, and the public tours were gradually discontinued by the mid-1990s.

Architects and design students have demonstrated a keen and ongoing interest in the building, which has been the recipient of many national architectural awards. As of 2006, students from North Carolina State University's School of Design were still coming to study one of the few rhomboid buildings in the world. It has been featured in the *New York Times Magazine*, in *Time* and *Newsweek* magazines, and in

The building was first referred to as the "Service Center" to emphasize the Plan's commitment to customer service. Photo courtesy of BCBSNC archives.

The "Triune Towers" in front of the building depict three hands that symbolize the working relationship between subscribers, health care providers, and BCBSNC. Photo courtesy of BCBSNC archives.

design exhibits at New York's Museum of Modern Art.[19] The building's sleek shape has also prompted high-profile companies such as Toyota to use it as a backdrop for advertisements.

Over the Years

Although the building was designed to accommodate an estimated 10 to 15 years of company growth, by 1987 there were 1,435 employees within the sloped walls of the Service Center. Longtime employees Gerald White and Betsy Parker described the crowded conditions of the late 1980s vividly: "That's when we had some employees parked in the hallways to do their job on the second and third floors in Claims and Subscriber Services," White recalled.[20] "The parking lot was bursting at the seams;

you had to wait in line to go through the cafeteria because there were so many people, and the elevators were constantly full," Parker noted.[21]

The Plan's rapid growth during the late twentieth century prompted the search for additional space. By 1985, the idea of adding a second building behind the original Service Center was tabled. One by one, additional buildings at the Eastowne office complex across the boulevard were leased, and in 1988 they were purchased. By 1998, the new Customer Service Center was built in Durham, so the rhomboid building returned to its original identity as Corporate Headquarters.

In the decades since the building was first envisioned as a way to literally and symbolically bring the many different offices of the merged parent Plans into one central location, history has repeated itself. As of 2007, with Blue Cross and Blue Shield of North Carolina's unprecedented growth, the original Corporate Headquarters building is now one of 11 company sites scattered across the Research Triangle area. Once viewed as the ultramodern, dramatic announcement of the era of "New Blue," the building's rhomboid design remains an architectural anomaly and home of the state's leading health insurer.

Another seemingly minor, yet significant shift in identity took place in 1973: the plan changed its name from North Carolina Blue Cross and Blue Shield to Blue Cross and Blue Shield of North Carolina (BCBSNC).[10] But why?

Blue Plans nationwide were trying to compete more effectively with commercial health insurance carriers, but they faced the problems of variable quality at the local level and a lack of uniform medical benefits for national accounts. Members of Congress had even criticized some Plans for inconsistent performance in the administration of government programs, such as the Federal Employee Health Benefit Program and CHAMPUS. In an effort to appeal to national accounts, the BCA and its member Plans agreed to adopt a uniform naming convention in order to communicate a united national Blue identity and subordinate the local ones. Rose explained that they were trying to convince large employers, such as the auto industry, that "whatever benefits they contracted for with their union in Detroit would be delivered in Arizona or Florida or North Carolina or wherever they had workers."[11] The branding of the Blues began in earnest, as the BCA developed specific standards for how the text, color, and font of Blue Plan logos, marketing materials, and signage should be treated in order to be consistently recognizable anywhere in the country.

The name change was just one of many ways in which Blue Plans were adjusting to an increasingly competitive marketplace. Although the rating practices of the commercial carriers had been influencing the direction of the health insurance industry since the 1950s, by the early 1970s the Blues had little choice but to surrender community ratings and employ experience ratings if they were to retain their subscribers and employer groups. Rose recalled: "The commercial insurance industry came along and stripped out all the bells and whistles that we were offering and were able to offer health coverage in a competitive way much less expensively than we were. So we had to go into experience rating, which was probably the biggest obstruction to upholding the idea of social purpose we had long held."[12] Another of the Plan's primary competitive strategies was to offer Administrative Services Only (ASO) contracts to many of its largest employer groups, such as IBM, R. J. Reynolds Tobacco, and the State of North Carolina. With an ASO, the employer assumed all of the risk of its group and none of the risk of other groups, which they had

1972

Recombinant DNA (rDNA) technology is first developed in 1972, giving rise to today's biotechnology industry.

In the early 1970s new medical imaging technologies—CAT, MRI, and PET scans—revolutionize medical practice, greatly reducing the need for exploratory surgeries.

In 1972, North Carolina creates a network of nine regional Area Health Education Centers (AHECs), one of the nation's first such programs.

The concept of outpatient surgery was a novel cost containment measure in the 1970s. Photo courtesy of BCBSNC archives.

been previously absorbing in part. Although both ASOs and experience ratings proved to be very popular offerings during this period, they also diminished the Plan's ability to spread some of the risk of groups with poor ratings across a larger pool of payers.

In addition to the increasing use of ASOs, experience ratings, and outpatient surgery as cost containment measures, Blue Plans also intensified their utilization review practices. BCBSNC had begun its utilization review activities in 1970 and expanded their scope by publishing manuals such as *Cost Containment Programs for Hospitals* and hosting utilization review seminars to expand providers' understanding of benefits and to discourage unnecessary hospitalizations. Claims review, with the aid of new computer programs that could screen for anomalies in utilization, began to save BCBSNC millions of dollars. Such tight control of utilization was one of the hallmarks of the HMO model, which was gaining momentum in the health care sector nationally, largely based on success stories generated by the Kaiser Permanente system in California and the Nixon administration's support. HMOs promised and rewarded efficiency, providing a market-based solution to the cost control crisis.

In 1973, Congress passed the Health Maintenance Organization Act, which provided federal grant and loan money to help launch new HMOs. Employers would now be required to offer coverage from at least one federally qualified HMO to all employees so that they had at least a dual choice. Though this requirement was never enforced, it did lend credibility to the HMO movement. The Nixon health care plan was a decidedly aggressive move in favor of this alternative delivery model, calling for a staggering increase from 30 to 1,700 HMOs by the end of the decade and an ambitious goal of having an HMO alternative available for 90 percent of the U.S. population.

Yes, No, Maybe

Although concern about the financing and delivery of health care was rampant and increased the pressure on Blue Plans to better control costs, the goal of developing widespread HMOs remained elusive. If Blue Plans had embraced the HMO concept and moved quickly to implement them, they could have made significant gains on the commercial carriers. But they—and the market overall—were slow to respond for several reasons. First, many physicians were highly resistant to the HMO model. The American Medical Association feared that it would lead to socialized medicine and vigorously opposed HMO-related legislation, as did many state medical societies. They felt that the emphasis on cost savings could

inhibit their freedom to make sound medical decisions and would create new administrative burdens on their office staffs. In addition, the system of health care delivery was—and is—massive, intricate, and far from nimble when rapid change is needed.

On the other side of the equation, the general public demonstrated mixed emotions about the growth of HMOs, from confusion and hopefulness to outrage and uncertainty. People wanted their health insurance premiums and out-of-pocket medical expenses reduced, but they also wanted the freedom to choose their doctor and receive the best of care. With the exception of those enrolled in the Kaiser system in the West, traditional fee-for-service relationships between physicians and their patients had, after all, been the only health care delivery system that most Americans at that time had ever known. Faced with such significant change, physicians and subscribers alike were slow to adopt the idea. By 1975, only 28 Blue Plans had developed HMOs. In North Carolina, although the Plan became federally qualified for incentives under the HMO Act, it would be another six years before the market indicated serious interest in this alternative method of delivery and BCBSNC responded.

The Supreme Court's 1973 decision in the case of *Roe v. Wade* legalizes abortion in the United States.

In 1973, Congress passes the Health Maintenance Organization Act, which provides federal grant and loan money to help launch new HMOs.

North Carolina passes hallmark legislation licensing nurses to perform medical acts and prescribe medications in 1975, improving access to health care for many.

As Americans celebrated the bicentennial in 1976, a mysterious respiratory disease struck attendees of the American Legion conference in Philadelphia. "Legionnaire's disease" was an early portent of new killer infectious diseases to come. Photo courtesy of the American Legion.

While the Nixon administration had garnered some support for the shift toward HMOs as a cost containment strategy, the overall national economy was also struggling with growing inflation in all major sectors. As a result, Nixon imposed wage and price controls in 1971 and again in 1973, but they did not achieve the intended results and were lifted in 1974. Health care costs immediately shot skyward, with hospital charges increasing by 16 percent and physician fees by 10 percent. Major medical coverage was an industry program developed to control costs, and the changes in its coverage limits matched the trajectory of costs during this decade—from a $40,000 maximum in 1968, to $250,000 in 1975, to $1,000,000 in 1980.[13]

In North Carolina, the costs of medical care doubled between 1974 and 1980. BCBSNC addressed these increases not only by seeking savings through cost containment measures such as utilization and claims reviews but also by raising revenues through rate increases. In 1975 it introduced catastrophic major medical coverage, which was quickly adopted by many groups. That same year, the Plan filed for rate increases averaging 25.6 percent for all four categories of its nongroup subscribers. But the state insurance commissioner approved increases less than those requested, so the Plan had to work even harder to find strategies for managing costs.

Hospital reimbursement rates were a constant concern to BCBSNC during this period and led to lengthy and difficult contract negotiations over the three-year period from 1975 to 1978. Because hospitals were reimbursed on the basis of their costs, they had a natural incentive to maximize rather than reduce costs in order to sustain their incomes. Without limits on hospital reimbursement claims, a Plan could easily become financially unstable, even insolvent, very quickly. Rose recognized that BCBSNC needed to develop a hospital contract that would include three new but necessary provisions. First, the contract would clearly identify the specific costs that the Plan would be willing to pay for, such as bad debts and depreciations but excluding research. Since hospital profits had previously ranged widely, the contract would now place a 5 percent cap on the profit margin. And finally, there would be agreement that the negotiated price would last for an annual period. Hospitals considered these contract elements very controversial and resisted them vigorously, particularly since the commercial carriers were not insisting on such provisions. Because of these protests, more than 30 drafts of the contract had to be prepared before agreement could be reached. Meanwhile, commercial carriers were increasingly challenging the pricing advantage inherent in the Blues' tax-exempt status and urging state legislatures to impose premium taxes on them, leading to intense advocacy efforts by BCBSNC's Governmental Affairs staff.[14]

Planning and Politics

Pressures for more efficiencies and related cost savings were driven not only by the bottom line but also from the national Blue Cross Association (BCA) and National Association of Blue Shield Plans (NABSP). Government programs such as Medicare and the Federal Employees Health Benefits Program (FEHBP) were contracted directly to the national associations, which then subcontracted to individual Plans such as BCBSNC for benefits administration. As a result, the Plans had accountability to the Associations for their performance as intermediaries for the government programs. In a decided break from the tradition of local operational autonomy, BCA and NABSP implemented an oversight activity known as Total Plan Review (TPR). A team of 40 Association officials conducted such a review of BCBSNC in 1975, analyzing each operational area for potential improvements. Their findings suggested that BCBSNC could improve by shifting from "task-oriented" to "results-oriented" planning processes, now a hallmark of contemporary best practices in business management. Tom Rose, still new in his role as president of BCBSNC, was open to their guidance and

implemented many of the TPR recommendations. But he candidly disclosed that many of his counterparts around the country highly resented the process, eventually resulting in the Association Plan review leader being fired.[15]

Improvements in planning included efforts to strengthen relationships with Plan subscribers as well. In 1975, BCBSNC formed 11 Subscriber Advisory Councils to continually assess the needs of its members and to receive regular feedback about current and proposed products and services. As with the public members of the Plan's board, the 12 to 15 members of each council had no direct affiliation with the health care industry and reflected the demographics of their area. BCBSNC was one of only 16 Plans in the country utilizing Subscriber Advisory Councils at that time, acting as an early model of how to involve consumers in management's strategic planning process.

Perhaps the most significant planning commitment that BCBSNC made during the 1970s was to install Long Range Systems Plan (LRSP)—a sophisticated data processing system designed by the BCA and NABSP. Participating Blue Plans employed LRSP to manage and integrate all data-driven business functions:

1975

1976

Although vaccinations and antibiotics had brought many infectious diseases under control, the mid-1970s saw the outbreak of new threats.

Tick-borne Lyme disease emerges and spreads rapidly.

In 1976, American Legion convention attendees are struck by the mysterious "Legionnaire's disease."

The dreaded Ebola virus hits several African countries with a vengeance.

In 1976, the Ford administration plans to vaccinate every American against a new strain of influenza known as swine flu.

claims payment and adjudication, billing, provider payment, payment reconciliation and utilization review. The system was actually a set of 10 product packages that were implemented over the four years from 1975 to 1979. LRSP not only allowed claims to be processed less expensively but kept providers and subscribers better informed about the status of their claims.

On the Threshold of National Health Insurance

The LRSP system was certainly intended to improve operational efficiency, but it also reflected major political developments. Although the debate about national health insurance had waxed and waned over the decades, the 1970s would prove to be the time when it came closest to being enacted. Democrats had long been the champions of a national health insurance for primarily social reasons. But with the surge in health care inflation and evidence of widespread Medicaid fraud and Medicare overspending, many Republicans who had long opposed the idea found sound business reasons to favor some form of it. In 1971, Senator Edward Kennedy of Massachusetts, a longtime proponent of health care reform, had been appointed chairman of the Senate health subcommittee, enhancing his ability to champion the cause of compulsory coverage for all Americans. The Kennedy plan, as well as a number of other competing proposals for national health insurance, was under

The New York Times

"All the News That's Fit to Print"

The New York Times

LATE CITY EDITION

Weather: Partly cloudy today; cool tonight. Fair, pleasant tomorrow. Temp. range: today 65-78; Thursday 64-85. Highest Temp.-Hum. Index yesterday: 75. Details on Page 66.

VOL. CXXIII..No. 42,566   © 1974 The New York Times Company   NEW YORK, FRIDAY, AUGUST 9, 1974   20¢ beyond 50-mile radius of New York City except Long Island. Higher in air delivery cities   15 CENTS

NIXON RESIGNS

HE URGES A TIME OF 'HEALING'; FORD WILL TAKE OFFICE TODAY

'Sacrifice' Is Praised; Kissinger to Remain

By ANTHONY RIPLEY
Special to The New York Times

WASHINGTON, Aug. 8—I will pledge to you tomorrow Vice President Ford praised President Nixon tonight for "one of the greatest personal sacrifices for the country and one of the finest personal decisions of all of us as Americans."

Mr. Ford, who will take office as the 38th President at noon tomorrow, vowed to continue Mr. Nixon's foreign policy and announced that Secretary of State Kissinger had agreed to stay on in the new Administration.

"I pledge to you tonight, as

SPECULATION RIFE ON VICE PRESIDENT

Some Ford Associates Say Selecting a Successor Could Take Weeks

By CHRISTOPHER LYDON
Special to The New York Times

The 37th President Is First to Quit Post

By JOHN HERBERS
Special to The New York Times

WASHINGTON, Aug. 8—Richard Milhous Nixon, the 37th President of the United States, announced tonight that he had given up his long and arduous fight to remain in office and would resign, effective at noon tomorrow.

At that hour, Gerald Rudolph Ford, whom Mr. Nixon nominated for Vice President last Oct. 12, will be sworn in as the 38th President, to serve out the 895 days remaining in Mr. Nixon's second term.

Less that two years after his landslide re-election victory, Mr. Nixon, in a conciliatory address on national

Text of the address will be found on Page 2.

television, said that he was leaving not with a sense of bitterness but with a hope that his departure would start a "process of healing that is so desperately needed in America."

He spoke of regret for any "injuries" done "in the course of the events that led to this decision." He acknowledged that some of his judgments had been wrong.

The 61-year-old Mr. Nixon, appearing calm and resigned to his fate as a victim of the Watergate scandal, became the first President in the history of the Republic to resign from office. Only 10 months earlier Spiro Agnew resigned the Vice-Presidency.

Speaks of Pain at Yielding Post

Mr. Nixon, speaking from the Oval Office, where his successor will be sworn in tomorrow, may well have delivered his most effective speech since the Watergate

Vice President Ford meeting with newsmen last night — The New York Times/William E. Sauro

President Nixon on TV as he announced his resignation — United Press International

POLITICAL SCENE SHARPLY ALTERED
Text of Mr. Ford's remarks appears on Page 3.
Avenue near the White House. Applause rang out from the crowds when Mr. Ford appeared briefly.
G.O.P. Prospects Improved

Rise and Fall
Appraisal of Nixon Career
By ROBERT B. SEMPLE Jr.

JAWORSKI ASSERTS NO DEAL WAS MADE
Save Nixon Did Not Ask for

President Nixon declared a health care crisis when he took office in 1969. But the Watergate scandal, which led to his 1974 resignation, effectively derailed progress toward federal health care reform at that time. Photo courtesy of the New York Times.

consideration in the early 1970s, all of which encouraged alternative delivery systems such as HMOs. By 1974, consensus was developing in Congress about the major features of a national health insurance program, and the enactment of major legislation was considered a foregone conclusion.[16]

Leaders at the BCA and NABSP engaged in extensive strategic planning in preparation for what was regarded as the inevitable adoption of national health insurance. A central feature of their readiness strategy included LRSP, which was specifically designed so that the Plans could implement national health insurance legislation more easily.[17] BCBSNC was an early adopter of the ambitious data processing system and was selected as one of the initial beta field-test sites. But the unfolding Watergate scandal, which ultimately led to Nixon's resignation in 1974, effectively undermined any chance for substantive advances in health care reform at that time. President Ford resumed reform efforts in August 1974, urging Congress to reach a compromise on the issue of national health insurance. But a series of close congressional votes on financing that month revealed a failure of consensus. This would prove to be the blow from which the "certainty" of national health insurance never recovered, although at that time it seemed only a temporary setback. During his brief presidency, Gerald Ford's domestic agenda then focused primarily on fighting the economic recession.

Subsequently, President Jimmy Carter sup-

ported the idea of national health insurance but would not endorse Senator Kennedy's 1978 comprehensive proposal; his administration made only more general efforts at cost containment. Despite the fact that national health insurance never got sufficient political traction, BCA leaders used the prospect of it to leverage much-needed Plan improvements through the Total Plan Review process and LRSP's cutting-edge data processing capabilities. Throughout this period, BCBSNC remained responsive to how political developments might impact business demands, adopting management practices and technical processes that could help sustain the Plan in an increasingly uncertain market.

A New Strategy

By the mid-1970s, the U.S. health care market was largely saturated, with 90 percent of the population insured. In 1975, Blue Cross Plans nationwide had 87 million subscribers, and BCBSNC was the 13th largest Plan among them, with 2.3 million subscribers. Unlike markets in many other areas of the country, the North Carolina health care insurance market still had room for growth, and BCBSNC was intent on reaching even more of those who needed access to affordable coverage. The Plan continued to make steady enrollment gains, in large part because of the renewal and expansion of the contract to provide benefits for teachers and state employees, making it the biggest contract in

In 1977, BCBSNC began to promote health education in order to improve patient outcomes and fight rising health care costs. Construction of the "LifeCourse" fitness trail around the perimeter of the BCBSNC grounds that same year reinforced this preventive strategy for the Plan's own employees. Photo courtesy of BCBSNC archives.

the Plan's history. Overall, Blue Cross and Blue Shield of North Carolina's membership increased 37 percent over the decade, with the company insuring approximately 35 percent of the state's population.

As fortunate as BCBSNC was to experience such continued growth, the conundrum of how to contain costs only grew worse. By 1977, the Plan was forced to increase rates again in order to avoid losses and a depletion of the required reserves. In addition to the ongoing efforts to intensify utilization review practices and host more workshops for benefits administrators, a new strategy emerged that would fight costs from a proactive stance—health education. The national Blue Cross and Blue Shield advertising campaign's theme—"If we all take care of ourselves, we're going to need less health care"—captured the idea that a focus on individual responsibility for health could have a significant positive impact on health care costs.

Locally, BCBSNC embarked on several new programs of health education. The Plan joined the President's Council on Physical Fitness and Sports in encouraging high school students to become more active in sports. It also promoted the immunization of school children through the Health and Education United (HEED) program. Groups were educated and screened for diseases such as cancer and diabetes through the Education and Screening Examination (EASE), starting with 500 of the Plan's own employees and a pilot group of 10,000 state employees in 1977. A new quarterly health education newsletter, HealthWise, was distributed to thousands of health care clinics and medical offices. Posters promoting good health practices were offered to all enrolled groups. At the northeast corner of the Service Center grounds, a .6-mile fitness trail known as the "LifeCourse" was developed to promote on-site exercise for employees. BCBSNC was the first company in North Carolina—and the first Blue Plan in the nation—to construct a fitness trail, becoming an early model of health-conscious business practices.

A Microcosm of the Larger Culture

The 1970s saw the beginning of the "fitness craze" that remains so much a part of our culture today. Americans were increasingly working out, and activities at BCBSNC reflected this trend, from the use of the LifeCourse to exercise classes held in the auditorium after work. Other signs of the social trends of the times were evident at the Plan too. As women became a larger part of the overall workforce, issues addressed by the women's liberation movement, such as the "glass ceiling," became part of the company dialogue. In a small informal 1971 internal survey, over half of the women at BCBSNC expressed the belief that they were discriminated against in regard to their pay. Company dress codes attempted to moderate fashion trends such as micro miniskirts and hip-hugger pants. Articles in the Plan's in-house magazine Bluebird explored the challenges of working mothers and featured women serving in the role of security guards, declaring that "women's lib is the last thing on their minds."[18] The heated debate over the use of racial and gender quotas through affirmative action resulted in greater scrutiny of hiring practices, and minority employment continually increased as the Plan grew.

Although advances in technology resulted in greater operational efficiencies, at times they also resulted in displaced employees. In 1972, member information was still kept on index cards and claims were reviewed manually. Claims allowances were processed on calculators and then sent to operators who entered the information on punch cards later processed by IBM keypunch machines. By 1975, member information could be accessed on cathode ray tube computer displays, regarded as a technical marvel at that time. Soon the keypunch operators became obsolete as data was entered directly into computer terminals that were part of large mainframe operating systems. By 1979, BCBSNC received the first electronic claim transmitted directly from Wilson Memorial Hospital, marking the beginning of the provider communication system.[19]

The 1970s witnessed a shift from decades in which Blue Cross and Blue Shield of North Carolina had experienced certain growth and wide-open markets to a new age of unprecedented rising health care costs and the promise of a new delivery model known as the HMO. By the end of the 1970s, managed care was still a small part of the U.S. health care system, with only 5 percent of Americans enrolled in prepaid arrangements such as HMOs.[20] But the pace of enrollment would begin to speed up in the 1980s as health care costs continued their seemingly uncontrollable upward spiral and employers saw HMOs as a way to manage those costs. The debate over national health insurance, once a near certainty, would become a more difficult uphill battle for its leading proponent, Senator Edward Kennedy. Under the new leadership of Plan President Tom Rose, BCBSNC continued to grow and adapt to radical changes in the health care market, from its financing and delivery to technology and the demographics of its workforce. Industry pressures would only increase in the coming decade, as HMOs found a foothold and consumers became more discriminating in their health care choices. Even so, as in every decade since the Plan's inception, more North Carolinians continued to find affordable health care coverage from BCBSNC than from any other insurer.

In 1979 the World Health Organization certified the worldwide eradication of smallpox, achieved through a combination of quarantines and vaccination. Photo courtesy of the World Health Organization.

1977

BCBSNC first launches prevention-based health education programs and screenings in 1977.

1978

The newly developed in vitro fertilization technique produces the first "test-tube baby" in 1978, generating intense ethical controversy about the procedure.

1979

In 1979, the World Health Organization certifies the worldwide eradication of smallpox, achieved by a combination of quarantines and vaccination.

Chapter Six

The Changing Health Care Landscape

Reform Needed—But What and How?

By the end of the 1970s, the movement toward enacting national health insurance lost momentum for lack of clear political support from the administration of President Jimmy Carter. In his 1976 campaign, Carter had assured Americans that he favored a comprehensive health insurance program, but seriously rising inflation undermined his economic domestic policy plans.[1] But once President Carter's proposal to stem rising health care costs by capping hospital rate increases went forward, it was met with hostility by the hospital industry and the measure died in the House. Congress also found it difficult to consider the massive spending that would

be required by a national health care program, which was seen as a force that would only aggravate inflationary pressure.

Furthermore, competing proposals for health care reform continued to be debated, eroding any hope for consensus passage of a national health insurance bill. Nevertheless, Senator Edward Kennedy persevered in what would continue to be an uphill battle on the issue, relentlessly pursuing a national health care agenda. In fact, he used it as a springboard from which to

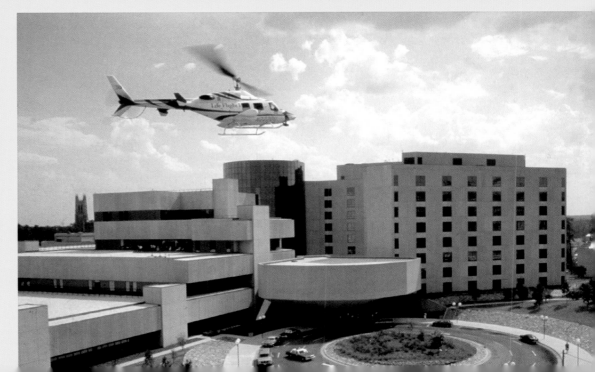

A Life Flight helicopter bound for Duke Hospital. Long known as "Bull Durham," in 1982 Durham declared its new identity as the "City of Medicine" when health care overtook tobacco as its leading industry. Photo courtesy of the City of Durham.

challenge President Carter, unsuccessfully, for the Democratic presidential nomination in 1980. But the numerous late-term crises faced by the Carter administration—an energy shortage, the Soviet invasion of Afghanistan, American hostages held by Iranian revolutionaries—paved the way for an overwhelming victory by Ronald Reagan in the 1980 presidential election. A significant change in political direction was about to take place.

In North Carolina, the traditional economic base was also changing. With growing scientific evidence about the hazards of smoking, cigarette use was declining, as was the state's once-dominant tobacco crop. The textile industry was also in crisis; many large plants were being closed. Ever since the Research Triangle Park began to develop in the 1960s, the state's largely rural population and agricultural economy had been evolving to embrace new industries in the research, medical, technical, and service sectors. This shift was evident in the City of Durham's decision to change its identity from the informal but historically resonant "Bull Durham" to the more contemporary "City of Medicine" (see *A Sign of the Times*). In keeping with these trends, BCBSNC was working hard to adapt its products to meet the health insurance needs of large employers in these newer economic sectors while continuing to offer coverage at lower costs to the diminishing and displaced rural population it had long served.

Managed Care Gains Traction in the Health Care Market

Another fundamental shift was about to take place in the state's health care market. Although HMOs were flourishing in some areas of the country—particularly the Kaiser system in the West—the overall numbers remained relatively small. By 1979, there were only 217 HMOs in the United States, compared to the 1,700 the Nixon health plan had called for by the end of the decade.[3] The Southeast was a particularly slow adopter, with less than 1 percent of the population enrolled in HMOs by 1980, compared to 4 percent of the nation's overall population.[4] In 1981, BCBSNC still lacked an HMO product. Instead, it offered comprehensive major medical coverage for the first time as a strategy to reduce costs, and the product immediately soared in sales. Meanwhile, other health insurers were competing aggressively, and the Plan suffered a major blow in 1982 when it lost the North

In 1980, the average life expectancy in the United States is 73.7 years. In North Carolina, the numbers for men are significantly worse: 70.2 years for white males, and only 63.6 for nonwhite males—a full ten years lower than the national average. The numbers for women are encouraging, with white women expected to live until 78.5, although nonwhite women are only expected to live 73.6 years.

By the 1980s, scientists have finally made a definitive connection between heart disease and lifestyle factors such as diet, cholesterol, and exercise levels. A new emphasis in health care then emerges—preventive medicine and the risk factor approach, which looks at how individuals contribute to disease.

Carolina Teachers' and State Employees' contract (see *I Remember: "The saddest day . . . the happiest day . . ."*). The loss yielded an almost 10 percent decline in market share and caused company leaders to reevaluate programs and priorities and to trim the workforce—a rare occurrence in BCBSNC's history.[5] A boost was needed, and a new product was about to provide it.

As the 1980s unfolded, both market conditions and the political climate under Reagan became optimal for HMO expansion. Cost containment strategies had failed. Liberal reform efforts had floundered. Consumers were becoming more accepting of the HMO concept. And employers were seeing HMOs as an attractive alternative in the face of still-rising hospital costs and insurance premiums. Conservatives had grown wary of government solutions and began to coalesce around the belief that a free market could effect the necessary cost containment and offer consumers a range of choices. Noted health care historian Paul Starr characterized the "conservative revelation" that would guide the health care reform strategies of the 1980s: "The problems of health care in America could be cured by relying on competition and incentives, if only government's role were reduced to a minimum."[7]

Corporations began to integrate the hospital system (previously a decentralized structure), enter many other health care–related businesses, and consolidate control. HMOs were now regarded as a field ripe for business development, and the trend toward commercialization rapidly

---

I Remember: "The saddest day . . . the happiest day . . . "

Thomas (Tom) A. Rose served as president of Blue Cross and Blue Shield of North Carolina for 20 years, from 1973 to 1993. When asked about the most significant business challenge he faced during that period, Rose recalled: "The really big one was in 1982 when we lost the account for the State of North Carolina. That was probably the saddest day of my life while I was at Blue Cross. I think that we had taken that account a little bit for granted and that we thought nobody could do it like we could. I think the mistake we made in that whole situation was that we did not submit our bid completely in accordance with the specifications.

"Probably the most thrilling and happiest day of my life was the day five years later when we got it back because of a number of reasons. The company that won the account from us in the first place was not very good at doing it, and there were change orders galore. The state employees and the governor were very unhappy with their service. Secondly, I think the legislature realized that what we had provided them earlier was superb service at a reasonable cost. They were delighted to have us take over the account again, and apparently have been very happy with the service of the company since then because we still have the account."[6]

A Sign of the Times

Durham had long been known as "Bull Durham" —home to tobacco factories and tobacco fortunes. But in 1980, BCBSNC conducted a study of the discharge records of Durham's five hospitals. The findings revealed that Durham hospitals, particularly the Duke University Medical Center, were playing a prominent role in the state and the region as major medical referral centers.

Soon after the study was released, a group of Durham's leading citizens began a grassroots campaign to have medicine and health care recognized as the city's greatest asset. Business and city government leaders, as well as area physicians, endorsed the idea and began fundraising to support what some would see as an upgrade in Durham's image, a radical break from its historic pride in tobacco manufacturing. BCBSNC assisted with the "City of Medicine" campaign kickoff by sponsoring a breakfast at the Service Center in January 1981. By 1982, Durham had proudly proclaimed

itself the City of Medicine USA, and its identity as Bull Durham would linger only in memories, history books, the ballpark, and the movies.[2]

accelerated. A profusion of both newly formed corporations and established insurers such as Prudential began to enter the HMO market, as did several Blue Cross and Blue Shield Plans. In North Carolina, BCBSNC President Tom Rose recognized that the Plan needed to consider alternative delivery systems. He recalled, "Our major customers were coming to us and saying, 'We want to try this HMO thing.'"[8] So in the spring of 1980, the Plan invited more than 300 representatives of business, industry, health professions, and government to a symposium in order to explore alternative means of delivering and financing health care in the state. Rose and his team then consulted with John Mannix, renowned Blue Cross leader from the Cleveland Plan, to create BCBSNC's first HMO offering: the Personal Care Plan[SM].[9]

The Personal Care Plan (PCP) was an individual practice association (IPA), an HMO model in which a contractual arrangement is made with physicians in private practice for the prepayment of medical services for enrolled subscribers. It was designed to limit increases in health care costs by emphasizing preventive care, maximizing ambulatory care, and reducing emergency care and hospitalization. The product offered much more comprehensive coverage than traditional health insurance, including benefits such as doctor's office visits and periodic physical examinations. It also provided financial incentives for both physicians and subscribers to deliver health care in the most cost-effective setting. BCBSNC

received its HMO license from the N.C. Department of Insurance on September 2, 1981.[10]

Much of 1981 was devoted to developing the marketing strategies, staff, and print materials to support promotion of the Personal Care Plan. Marketing activities began with the Plan's own employee group and other large enrolled groups in early 1982. By the end of that year, there were about 3,000 members enrolled in the Personal Care Plan. Although the high-level product design, benefits structure, and marketing strategies for the Personal Care Plan were in place and enrollment was gaining momentum, the specifics of implementation were considerably less clear.

One of the first implementation steps was to recruit both primary care physicians and specialists from the Research Triangle area as providers for the HMO. Among those recruited was Dr. Don Bradley, chief medical officer for BCBSNC, who at the time was a physician with a large primary care practice through the Duke Family Medicine Program. Bradley recalled that in the early days his practice seemed to know more about planning for and implementing an HMO product than the Plan did. "The Plan knew relatively little about what an HMO was supposed to be and really assumed we would take care of it. We set up a committee on how we were going to handle referrals and created our own office structure and database to take care of it. Quite frankly, it was somewhat more sophisticated than what I thought BCBSNC was doing at the time. That was the early intent of the HMOs, but there was virtually no guidance around that. There were very few rules written up. We almost ended up advising the staff at BCBSNC about how we were managing things."[11] By the end of 1982, more than 650 physicians had become part of the Personal Care Plan physician network. Their early experiences with this new model of health care financing and delivery yielded mixed levels of satisfaction within their practices and among their patients, and those feelings would only intensify as the HMO model gained traction.

The learning curve about how to successfully manage an HMO product was perhaps steeper because BCBSNC's first step was an ambitious one compared to that of many other insurers entering the market. As Bradley noted: "In retrospect, we did not go through a real evolution in managed care. The PPOs (preferred provider organizations) were designed to be an intermediate step—you have a network and yet you're still allowing patients to choose where they want to go. We skipped that step and moved right to a fairly draconian HMO model that required lots of prior Plan approval through a gatekeeper to reduce unnecessary care. Of course, there were some incentives and good reasons for doing that, not the least of which was uncontrolled rising

In 1981, the Centers for Disease Control and Prevention reported the first cases of a rare pneumonia and skin cancer in five young gay men in Los Angeles, California. These cases were later recognized as the first reported cases of AIDS in the United States. Since that time, AIDS has become one of the greatest public health challenges both nationally and globally. Photo courtesy of Time Inc.

1981

The first vaccine for hepatitis B is developed in 1981.

Collaboration between a mechanical engineer and a trauma surgeon results in the development of artificial skin. It is first used to treat a third-degree burn in 1981.

In 1981, the "AIDS virus" (identified in 1983 as HIV) is first detected.

1982

In 1982, Durham, N.C., proudly proclaims itself the City of Medicine USA, reflecting its leading role in state and regional health care.

Advances in computer technology enabled the first paperless claims transmission in 1983. The number of claims would triple over the next 10 years. Photo courtesy of BCBSNC archives.

health care costs."[12] Health care financing needed a course correction, and HMOs were regarded as one major solution.

The Pain and the Promise of Change

Other changes quickly followed. Not long after he entered office in 1981, President Reagan launched an aggressive effort to reform the federal health care system, announcing plans to consolidate all 26 health services programs into two block grants, one for health services and the other for preventive health. A committed conservative, Reagan declared his intention to slash federal spending on health by 25 percent. As the single largest purchaser of health services, the government had tremendous power to influence cost containment. In 1982, Congress passed the Tax Equity and Fiscal Responsibility Act, which called for development of a prospective system for Medicare to tighten regulations and establish reimbursement rates. Previously, payment for Medicare services had been administered on a treatment basis, but in a prospective system payment would instead be based on diagnosis. Patient treatment and specific reimbursement rates would now be driven by a new classification system of 470 "diagnosis-related groups" (DRGs) organized into 23 major diagnostic categories. The system also factored in numerous patient and hospital variables, such as age, gender, complications, hospital location, patient loads, and teaching activity.

President Reagan signed the Medicare Prospective Payment System (PPS) legislation into effect in April 1983. Once this system became operative, the number of Medicare patients fell rapidly, and the rate of increase in Medicare expenditures dropped significantly, yielding savings in the millions. However, PPS was not a simple success story. Ongoing concerns about the quality of care stemmed from a perception that patients were discharged "quicker and sicker." DRGs were also complex to administer at hospitals and intermediaries alike. BCBSNC first used the new PPS reimbursement rate for Medicare beneficiaries in an aggressive effort to control the costs of inpatient services in acute care hospitals. This implementation of PPS resulted in particularly heavy workloads within Membership Services in 1983.

The increased demand for health care services had been contributing to the Plan's steady growth, delivering the strongest year for group enrollment in over a decade. But that same growth also created a significant strain on its claims processing capabilities. In 1982, BCBSNC was processing almost 6 million claims, nearly 90 percent of which were still processed on the old, manual system. Conversion to a new, fully automated system was in the works, which was intended to yield greater accuracy, consistency, and efficiency in claims processing. But early in 1983, serious complications arose in the system conversion effort, resulting in a major backlog of claims and deterioration of service to subscribers.

Delays and errors drove increased subscriber inquiries, and the staff worked long hours to correct the issues.

The Plan was entering an age of operations that was increasingly integrated with new technologies. The first year the telephone system was fully computerized was 1983. By 1986, toll-free access was available for the first time to improve access for subscriber telephone inquiries.[13] More and more providers were also submitting their claims through a computer-based Provider Communication System, with 110 of the state's hospitals and 24 physician practices using the new paperless process. Computer terminals were now commonplace in physician and hospital offices and throughout BCBSNC. As the claims volume skyrocketed from 5.5 to 16 million between 1983 and 1992, the Plan continued to update its claims processing technology, while keeping the turnaround time required for processing to a reasonable standard of 14 days. With this growing level of demand, there was no doubt that development of the company's technical infrastructure would be a necessary and constant part of the Plan's operating budget for the foreseeable future.

Other aspects of the business were growing too. Group Insurance Services, Inc., the Plan's subsidiary offering life and disability insurance products, achieved the $1 billion mark in coverage in 1983, which tripled to $3 billion only two years later.[14]

In keeping with the national trend, health care costs were rising at a double-digit rate. While infectious diseases had been largely brought under control by the use of vaccinations, other illnesses such as cancer, heart disease, and stroke were now leading causes of death. These were increasingly being treated with new medical procedures, technologies, and drugs that often saved lives but were very expensive. In 1983 alone, the costs of inpatient hospitalization rose 17 percent, physician charges by 10 percent, and outpatient services by 14 percent. The Plan drew upon the expertise of its Office of Health Economics Research to investigate the state's hospital utilization patterns as a basis for considering alternative ways of delivering care and containing runaway costs. In 1983, after several years of research and analysis, the Health Economics Research staff released the findings of a statewide study that revealed wide discrepancies in hospital utilization rates and provider practice patterns among North Carolina counties. The study was highly publicized and

1982

The FDA issues tamper-resistant packing regulations in 1982 to prevent poisonings, such as deaths from cyanide placed in Tylenol capsules.

A miracle cardiovascular procedure takes place in 1982: the first artificial heart is implanted into patient Barney Clark. He lives 112 days.

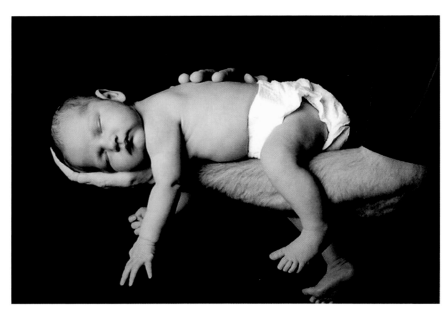

Baby delivered by a certified nurse-midwife, cradled on her father's arm. Certified nurse-midwives received recognition to practice in North Carolina in 1983. Photo courtesy of the American College of Nurse-Midwives.

led to a flood of requests by employers for similar studies of their utilization problems in order to identify and integrate cost containment features into their benefit programs.

This research influenced many of BCBSNC's cost containment initiatives in the early 1980s. Ambulatory surgery was strongly promoted, doubling in use from 1979 to 1982. The Plan also began an 18-month statewide pilot of the Office Surgery Incentive program in 1982. The program evaluated the effects of providing financial incentives to doctors for performing certain surgical procedures in their offices rather than hospitals. A program for preadmission certification—a standard practice in today's health care environment—was also first implemented in 1983 to address inappropriate and unnecessary hospital stays. Utilization review and coordination of benefits efforts were stepped up, and the CostWise® program was introduced to address the determination of benefit payments to doctors, which would now be limited by usual, customary, and reasonable allowances for covered services. Benefits and costs were examined at every level in an effort to lower the overall price tag of health care.

1983

In 1983, certified nurse-midwives receive recognition to practice in North Carolina. Once viewed as contributors to maternal mortality, midwives now improve the health of mothers and babies at birth.

By 1983, U.S. health care costs are rising at a double-digit rate. In response, HMOs and other forms of "managed care" experience explosive growth. Between 1985 and 1990, national HMO enrollment grows from 19.1 to 33.3 million. North Carolina is slower to adopt managed care, as BCBSNC introduces its first HMO in 1981.

1984

In 1984, Congress passes the National Organ Transplant Act, allowing for the creation of national donor registries that help identify organ matches between unrelated donors and recipients.

Peaks . . .

The numbers started to turn around—dramatically. BCBSNC's cost containment programs quickly began to work. For example, the Pre-Admission Certification Program (PAC) experienced astronomical growth, expanding from 90,000 members in 1984 to more than 1 million in 1986. There was a 23 percent decrease in inpatient hospital admissions among those participating in PAC, resulting in more than 9 million dollars in savings for the Plan. Statewide use of ambulatory surgery tripled, saving members 20 million dollars. The same positive trend was evident on a national level. From 1980 to 1985, the rate of average annual increase in overall spending on health care dropped from almost 14 percent to less than 8 percent, driving a surge of optimism in the outlook for health spending.[15]

The popularity of HMOs was definitively on the rise as well, driving major changes in the utilization of medical services. The "gatekeeper" function and the addition of member copayments quickly acted as a deterrent to unnecessary care, yielding some of the desired cost savings for insurers and providers. The Plan had joined with HMOs in 20 other states to form a national network, HMO-USA®, which had a strong appeal to multistate employers. Enrollment in the Personal Care Plan (PCP) exceeded even national trends. In 1983, 30 percent of new BCBSNC members chose the PCP, compared to 8 to 10 percent nationally. Enrollment swelled

to 20,000 by the next year, then to more than 30,000 members in 1985. Given its phenomenal success, the PCP program, now the flagship product, became a federally qualified HMO in 1986 and was established as a wholly owned, for-profit subsidiary. This enabled it to meet even greater market demand and remain competitive in an exploding HMO market. Recognizing the opportunity to diversify its HMO products further, BCBSNC began development of a group practice, hospital-based HMO as another for-profit subsidiary.

The Plan also undertook the first steps toward

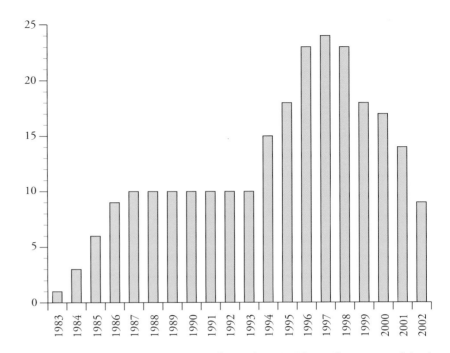

North Carolina HMO enrollment started slowly in the early 1980s, peaked in the late 1990s, then quickly and steeply declined. Graph courtesy of the North Carolina Department of Insurance.

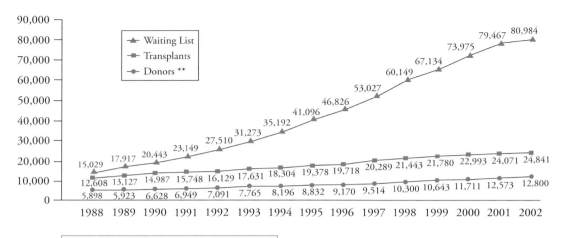

90,000
80,000
70,000
60,000
50,000
40,000
30,000
20,000
10,000
0

- ▲ Waiting List
- ■ Transplants
- ● Donors **

1988 1989 1990 1991 1992 1993 1994 1995 1996 1997 1998 1999 2000 2001 2002

Waiting List: 15,029 17,917 20,443 23,149 27,510 31,273 35,192 41,096 46,826 53,027 60,149 67,134 73,975 79,467 80,984

Transplants: 12,608 13,127 14,987 15,748 16,129 17,631 18,304 19,378 19,718 20,289 21,443 21,780 22,993 24,071 24,841

Donors: 5,898 5,923 6,628 6,949 7,091 7,765 8,196 8,832 9,170 9,514 10,300 10,643 11,711 12,573 12,800

* Data from UNOS OPTN Scientific Registry
** Data include cadaveric and living donors

The 1984 National Organ Transplant Act created donor registries that help identify organ matches between unrelated donors and recipients. The serious shortage of organs available for transplants has worsened over time. Graph courtesy of the U. S. Department of Health and Human Services.

creating a preferred provider organization (PPO). In 1984, Valerie Carter, director of Corporate Planning, was tasked with studying PPOs. Carter recalled: "We stepped up our interest in PPOs primarily because the Catawba Memorial Hospital was under a lot of competitive pressure from an outrageously expensive for-profit facility in Hickory. Catawba came to our senior vice president, Dr. Stuart Sessoms, and asked if we would be interested in participating in a preferred provider organization. So we did more analysis and decided the best way to get started was to be sure we had the appropriate enabling legislation."[16] Once the needed state legislation was in place, BCBSNC decided to go forward with PPO products.

Returning to the Hickory area, Carter then launched a PPO pilot within a three-county area, sending out a request for proposals and creating an environment for bidding among the six area hospitals. She acknowledged that "it was very different from our normal way of doing business. The theory was that if you gave everybody an equal opportunity to bid and one bid lower than the other, presumably they would make up for the difference in the increased volume. So the Plan would have higher benefits at the preferred provider level and would be paying less for the services. So lo and behold, we set up the pilot and had this phenomenal bid."[17] Based on the success of the pilot, BCBSNC expanded its reach to other field regions with formal bidding dates, offering a conference in the middle of the bidding period to answer questions to prospective hospitals. Over the next five years, BCBSNC was the first insurer in the state to develop a statewide PPO network of preferred hospitals and doctors, known as Preferred Care.

BCBSNC recognized the promise of HMOs for managing what had seemed to be out-of-control health care costs and was now building on its success. Former BCBSNC President Tom Rose noted: "In 1986, our reserves got to the point where we thought they were at an excessive level. So our board of trustees said, 'Let's refund some of this money back to our customers.' We decided that we would take $75 million out of the reserves and through depressing the pricing of future coverage, we would in effect be giving discounts to refund this excess money."[18] Rose then informed the state Department of Insurance of the Plan's decision so that its officials would not become concerned about the change in reserves. The refund idea was realized in the Rate Stabilization Program, which resulted in rates 9 percent below what they would have been. More and more new products like vision care and a prescription drug card system were introduced in the mid- to late 1980s. The future looked bright.

. . . and Valleys

Or so it seemed. By the second half of the decade, the numbers were no longer adding up as hoped. The Personal Care Plan was consistently losing money, despite the skyward growth trend of its first few years. By 1985, the administrative staff for the HMO had doubled. Beginning in 1987 and continuing through 1988, the cost of claims rose at an alarming rate, both in North Carolina and in the nation at large. The 20 percent increase in claims paid from 1987 to 1988 was rapid, unexpected, and unprecedented. With concurrent payment of millions of dollars in refunds, the Plan experienced a double whammy—record-breaking losses and a 50 percent reduction in reserves. Similarly, BCBSNC

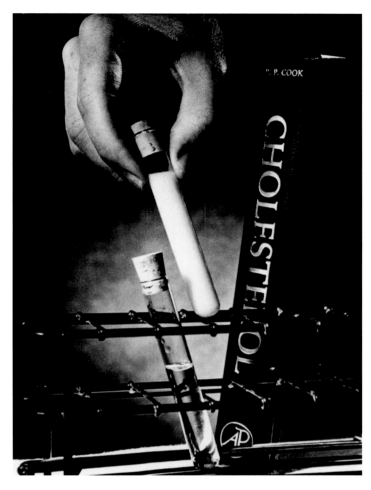

Research first distinguished between "good" and "bad" cholesterol in 1985. Blood plasma, normally clear, appears milky when cholesterol levels become too high. Photo by Jerry Hecht, courtesy of the World Health Organization and National Institutes of Health.

1985

In 1985, AIDS takes center stage. Ryan White, a teen with AIDS, is barred from school. Actor Rock Hudson dies from AIDS. The first International AIDS Conference is held in Atlanta. The disease is now declared a pandemic.

Prompted in part by the AIDS crisis, worldwide interest in immunology peaks in the mid-1980s. Research yields a new understanding of the structure and functioning of "helper" T-cells.

In 1985, research about cholesterol metabolism distinguishes between "good" (HDL) and "bad" (LDL) cholesterol, resulting in new approaches for the treatment and prevention of atherosclerosis (hardening of the arteries).

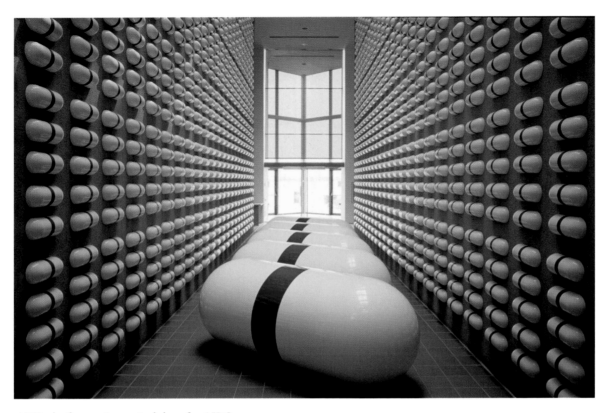

AZT, the first antiretroviral drug for AIDS, was developed by Burroughs-Wellcome in NC's Research Triangle Park in 1988. It became one of the first medications to effectively delay progression of the disease and replication of the virus. Pictured on the floor is one day's dosage of AZT. On the walls is one year's dosage. Photo courtesy of Collection General Idea.

subscribers experienced some of the highest rate increases ever—averaging 60 percent over the last six months of 1988. Although the rate of inflation in 1988 was an alarming 4.4 percent, it did not account for the superheated costs of health care. From 1985 to 1990, overall expenditures per consumer rose an astonishing 68 percent. What could possibly explain this unprecedented trend?

Certainly no single factor could account for the increases. Concern over rising health care costs had led providers and insurers to direct treatment in less costly settings whenever possible, as seen in the increased use of ambulatory surgery and the record number of visits people were making to doctors' offices and outpatient facilities. As a consequence, those entering the hospital for inpatient treatment were sicker. Both the Reagan administration and much of the general public had been slow to recognize the seriousness of the AIDS epidemic, allowing it to reach crisis proportions as the 1980s advanced. And there were other costly changes going on. One-third of all births were now by caesarean section, and there was a 22 percent rise in neonatal care services between 1985 and 1988. Advanced, expensive medical technologies were being used more routinely in all health care settings. As one example among many, the use of air ambulances to transport accident victims and seriously ill patients had grown significantly. While dramatically increasing the probability of survival, this type of transport was also driving up the costs of treating heart disease. There was an increasing gap between the cost of providing service to Medicare patients and the federal reimbursement payments.

Faced with these unprecedented trends, BCBSNC was unrelenting in its cost containment efforts. In order to place patients who required long-term care in the most cost-effective setting, personal benefits management was added to the Plan's managed care programs in 1987. A special fraud investigation department was added that same year to look into health insurance fraud and bring offenders to trial. Pre-Admission Certification, the Plan's most successful cost containment program, was extended in 1987 to nongroup subscribers as well as to employer groups. Physician participation in the CostWise program had grown to 67 percent, and contract negotiations with hospitals intensified.

While increasing enrollment in the Plan's HMO had seemed like a business boom, after only a few years it was proving to be a bust. As one study of the HMO industry found, efficiency gains tended to decrease as HMO size increased.[19] Dr. Bradley clearly recalled: "When I arrived in 1988, utilization of the Personal Care Plan was out of control. Mental health bed days were 90–100 for every 1,000 members per year—outlandish and not atypical of that time. The promise of managed care was that we would trim the unnecessary. By developing some guidelines, we were able to beat that down to 50–70 bed days. It was a significant reduction, but nowhere near what we anticipated that we would do."[20] BCBSNC then contracted with an external managed mental health care provider that was very intense in its management of care. As a result, BCBSNC was able to drive the number of mental health bed days down to the 30–35 range. But it took a couple of years to get the numbers under control.

Time for Triage

Other serious business decisions were necessary in order to abate the losses. Perhaps the most serious step taken to make the Personal Care Plan a more effective and financially sound program occurred in 1988, when Plan leaders decided to discontinue the bid for the North Carolina Teachers' and State Employees' contract. The pricing and specifications in the contract at that time made it impossible to administer in a fiscally responsible manner. This decision resulted in the loss of 40,000 Personal Care Plan members, most

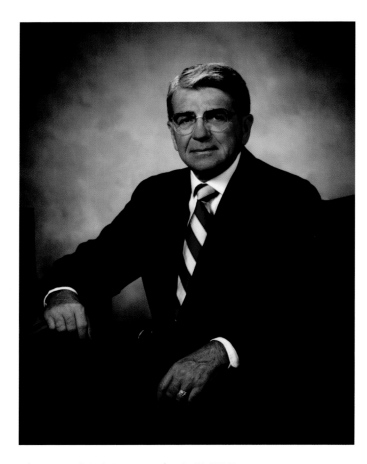

Thomas A. (Tom) Rose served as BCBSNC president during 20 critical years of stabilization and growth from 1973 to 1993. Photo courtesy of BCBSNC archives.

of whom transferred to more traditional coverage offered by BCBSNC. Undoubtedly, one of the most painful lessons learned during the early HMO years was summarized by Tom Rose: "You cannot administer an HMO program as inexpensively as you can traditional coverage. There is more cost associated with delivering that product than there is in delivering traditional coverage. Our board had to get used to that idea. We couldn't do HMO business at 4 and 5 percent of income as they'd been accustomed to."[21]

While the Personal Care Plan was being reevaluated, the HMO-NC program was expanding to the Charlotte area, and members were experiencing the lowest of all program rate increases. The Preferred Care PPO also continued to grow. These developments were testimony to the general instability and unpredictability of the managed care market overall during the late 1980s. Dr. Bradley recognized that "neither the insurance companies nor patients and physicians were prepared for the shock of moving that fast in a very short period of time."[22] As one product or health insurer was in the ascendancy, others were in decline. In fact, from 1986 through 1993, more than 200 HMOs left the national market through merger or business failure. Findings showed that smaller and

younger HMOs were more likely to be acquired or fail, while older, larger, and more profitable HMOs were more likely to acquire and survive.

Other new developments challenged the way the Blues traditionally conducted their business. The increasingly competitive market led some Blue Plans to engage in new practices, such as incorporating as mutual companies, creating subsidiaries, writing major medical coverage, and rating certain large employee groups based on their group experience. BCBSNC was among those using such innovative practices, having used experience rating and maintaining a thriving life insurance subsidiary, GIS, for decades as well as offering comprehensive major medical insurance since 1981. In addition, many of the new HMOs applied for tax-exempt status, and some received it.

Amid growing consumer and competitor protests, legal challenges, and government scrutiny, pressure mounted on the Internal Revenue Service to reconsider the tax status of Blue Plans. This ultimately led to reconsideration of the fundamental principles on which the tax-exempt status of Blue Plans was based. A study conducted by the U.S. Government Accounting Office in 1986 found that there were more similarities than differences between Blue Plans and commercial companies. The resulting Tax Reform Act of 1986 led to partial loss of the special tax status with the government that the Blues had enjoyed for decades.[23] On the positive side, once the tax laws changed, it opened the door even wider for Blue Plans to develop subsidiaries and even to consider conversion to for-profit status. On the negative side, BCBSNC was now a fully taxed business, making it more challenging to remain competitive as more managed care companies entered the market.

Recovery, for the Moment

Of course, not all of the trends and developments of the late 1980s were negative. A major business victory was winning back the North Carolina Teachers' and State Employees' contract in 1987 (See *I Remember: The saddest day . . . the happiest day . . .*). The Personal Care Plan did survive and was extensively restructured, primarily in its provider arrangements. In fact, the troubled HMO product ended 1989 in the black for the first time in its operating history. While continuing to exercise its cost containment efforts, BCBSNC was also becoming committed to the principle of offering consumers a range of choices through a growing portfolio of products. The Plan now had several managed care offerings—the PCP, PPO, and HMO-USA—to meet the different needs of individuals and employers. It also introduced Flexible Benefits Programs, which allowed employers to offer their employees premium conversions, flexible spending accounts, and cafeteria plans.

In keeping with its long-standing role as an insurer committed to expanding access to health care, in 1987 BCBSNC offered a consumer

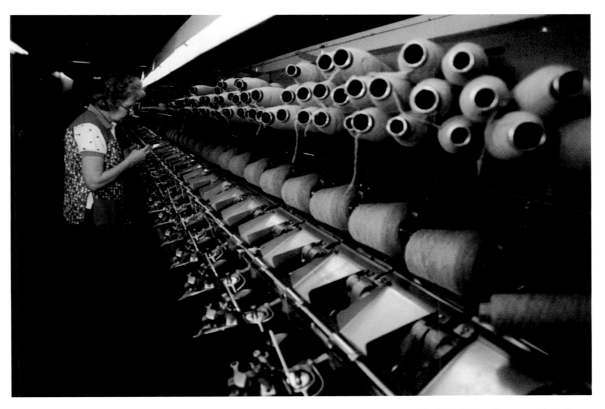

The North Carolina textile industry was in serious decline by the 1980s, leaving many unemployed and uninsured. Photo courtesy of BCBSNC archives.

program called SNAP, which was designed for people who could not otherwise obtain health care coverage. The Plan also agreed to underwrite The Caring Program for Children, which would provide coverage for children of low-income families in North Carolina who did not qualify for other assistance programs. But as important as developing new products and programs was to the recovery effort, BCBSNC also began to redefine its identity as a provider of health care coverage. Through extensive research, the Plan began to understand the need for radical redesign of health care delivery systems and its own role in developing favorable health care policies that would make health care more effective and more affordable.

The 1980s had been a roller-coaster decade in the health care landscape. The Plan celebrated its 50th anniversary in 1983, acknowledging its rich heritage of serving the state's health care needs since the birth of the Blue Cross concept itself. But in the midst of this accomplishment, BCBSNC leaders could hardly have foreseen the stellar growth of its first HMO product or the nearly catastrophic increases in claims and resultant financial losses that would come over the next few years. Nationally, enrollment in managed care plans had increased 400 percent in a decade, from 9 million in 1980 to 36 million in 1990. By the end of the decade, the BCBSNC staff had outgrown the Service Center in Chapel Hill. Given the financial uncertainty of the late 1980s, Tom Rose admitted that he did not favor building more buildings. So the Plan purchased five new buildings in 1988 that had previously been leased in the Eastowne office complex in Chapel Hill, the first purchase of space for expansion since 1973.[24]

As BCBSNC approached the 1990s, the Plan returned to a position of financial strength. Though enrollment had dropped, recovery had been driven by rate increases, and reserves were once again rising. But health care costs certainly had not stopped their upward climb. The next decade would only continue to test Blue Cross and Blue Shield of North Carolina's leadership, innovation, and competitive will to manage these rising costs while continuing to provide health care coverage for the state's increasingly diverse population.

1987

1988

In the mid-1980s, tuberculosis—thought to have been vanquished by antibiotics in the 1940s—begins to rise again. In a cruel twist, many patients now exhibit drug resistance brought on in part by the widespread use of antibiotics.

In 1988, AZT, the first antiretroviral drug for AIDS, is developed by Burroughs-Wellcome in North Carolina's Research Triangle Park and approved by the FDA.

Chapter Seven

Health Care in Crisis

In the Grip of Recession

During the 1980s, the free market approach to health care reform fueled the expansion of HMOs under President Reagan's administration. But by the end of the decade, foreign policy issues preoccupied the Reagan White House. From its outset in 1989, the presidency of George Bush, Sr., was also directed toward matters abroad, such as the U.S. invasion of Panama, the Gulf War, and collaboration with Soviet President Mikhail Gorbachev to create a "new world order" after the fall of communism in Eastern Europe. Federal policy toward health care lay dormant for several years, while managed care plans proliferated and costs continued to climb.

As the health care market tried to regain stability while experimenting with new kinds of delivery and financing, many cost containment strategies—diagnosis-related groups, utilization review, tighter controls over hospital reimbursement—achieved only temporary success. Savings in one area were countered by increased spending in another, and new cost categories were appearing with troubling regularity. The growing uninsured population was also driving up the costs of care. Rate increases were necessary in many Blue Plans to compensate for record losses. One of the hardest hit was Blue Cross and Blue Shield of West Virginia, which was unable to recover from its fiscal freefall and became the first Blue Plan to become insolvent and go out of business. It was a sobering wake-up call for Blue Plans nationwide and provoked a

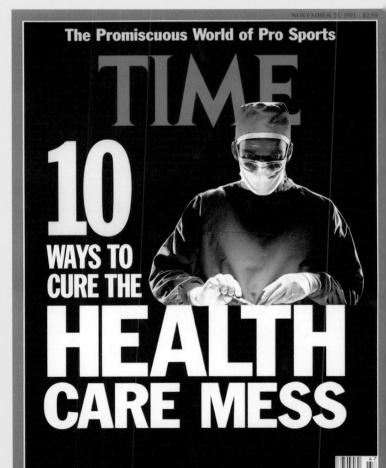

The health care market experienced a period of marked instability during the 1980s, prompted by new models of delivery and financing. Photo courtesy of Time Inc.

In 1991, BCBSNC broke ranks with other insurers and supported mandated benefits for annual mammograms. The company's breast health outreach efforts also included the button chair—each button given by a breast cancer survivor or victim—which ultimately became the focal point of a BCBSNC Foundation signature program (see pages 143–144 for more on the Foundation). Photo courtesy of BCBSNC archives.

public crisis of confidence in the Plans' viability as a system. In their long, proud history, the Blues had seemed invulnerable, and the public still did not fully understand that each Plan was actually a freestanding business entity.[1]

Blue Cross and Blue Shield of North Carolina was relying more and more on a growing portfolio of managed care offerings to ease financial challenges as it entered the 1990s. This dependence yielded uneven results. Although the popular but unprofitable Personal Care Plan had rebounded somewhat in 1989, it lost money again in 1990. Employers and consumers alike increasingly chose Preferred Care®, the PPO product that offered more benefit and provider options. As a result, the Plan expanded the product to statewide coverage in 1990. By 1991, the Plan's overall financial performance and growth had improved, as PPO group sales soared well beyond projections. A financial turnaround seemed to be in the making.

While striving to compete with national health insurers making inroads in the state's market, BCBSNC continued to consider how it could expand access for those with too little or no insurance at all. In 1991, the company offered two new products specifically for those who could not afford or were not eligible for existing types of coverage. The Access℠ program (which replaced the earlier SNAP product) was designed for people whose preexisting conditions often made it impossible for them to get health insurance from for-profit carriers. The other product, known as BasiCare℠, was the result of a unique product development process that targeted uninsured individuals or underserved small groups or individuals. Extensive focus groups were conducted to understand what the uninsured could afford and what coverage they most wanted for that amount. Despite this careful needs analysis and a major product launch, BasiCare failed to cover as many of those in need of affordable health insurance as had been hoped and was ultimately a disappointment. The uninsured population tended to purchase BasiCare for only brief periods to fill coverage gaps and eventually chose other competitors' products that offered similar pricing but greater benefits. Other adjustments to the product line were also made. Despite several product disappointments and an economic recession that had gripped the country since the late 1980s, by 1992 BCBSNC was experiencing its fourth straight year of growth.

1990

In 1990, the average life expectancy in the United States is 75.4 years. In North Carolina, the numbers remain lower: 72.2 years for white males, and only 64.9 for nonwhite males. Life expectancy for white women again exceeds the average, at 79.4 years, and nonwhite women are expected to live 74.5 years.

1991

With the rise in managed care, states increasingly mandate benefits for preventive care. In 1991, BCBSNC breaks ranks with other insurers and supports mandated benefits for annual mammograms.

New Leadership Brings New Vision

In 1992, the ongoing economic recession forced President Bush to renege on his famous pledge, "Read my lips: No new taxes," fueling a growing discontent with his leadership. In his campaign for reelection, Bush was confronted with two surprisingly strong contenders: Bill Clinton and Ross Perot. The relatively unknown and charismatic governor of Arkansas, Bill Clinton, campaigned on a platform of change in which the economy and health care reform figured prominently. Health care spending had, in fact, increased from 11.3 to 13.5 percent of the gross domestic product during the Bush administration.[2] Given this leap, health care was identified as a top concern of voters as the 1992 election approached. Clinton swept into office, enabling the Democrats to regain control of the presidency and both houses of Congress for the first time in 12 years.

As soon as President Clinton took office in January 1993, he appointed First Lady Hillary Rodham Clinton to head a task force charged with creating a comprehensive health care reform proposal that would deliver the campaign promise of affordable health care for all Americans. Major health care interest groups had endorsed the concept, if not the specifics, of substantial reform. Even the American Medical Association and the Health Insurance Association of America, two powerful entities

In 1993, First Lady Hillary Clinton, seen here with Surgeon General C. Everett Koop, led health care reform efforts that included universal health insurance. One year after the Clinton Health Security Act was introduced, it was soundly defeated. Photo courtesy of U.S. National Library of Medicine.

that had traditionally opposed compulsory health insurance, now publicly favored an employer mandate and universal coverage.[3] Initially, the time seemed ripe for enacting sweeping reform.

Although the early signs from the public and major stakeholder groups had been positive, the Clinton Health Security plan quickly lost momentum. During this first year in office, President Clinton turned his attention from the important to the urgent: from health care to the economy and the budget. The task force was to deliver its report in 100 days. It did not. Months rolled past as the group wrangled with the plan's proposed structure, costs, and benefits. The task force finally presented its report, known as the Health Security Act, to Congress in September 1993. The central feature of the Clinton plan was an enforced mandate for employers to provide health insurance coverage to all of their employees through competitive but closely regulated HMOs.

But the plan's complexity and economic calculations quickly allowed opponents to cast it as "big government-run insurance" that limited choice. The opposition—which now included many Republicans as well as some Democrats, the pharmaceutical industry, and the Association of Physicians and Surgeons—was gathering strength, and media coverage quickly eroded support for the plan.

During the following year, many other health care proposals were put forward by members of Congress in an effort to find a consensus position that had a chance of going forward. The national Blue Cross and Blue Shield Association (BCBSA) also introduced its own reform proposal, entitled *Community Partnerships for a Healthy America,* which outlined ways to revamp rather than dismantle the health care system, retaining its best features while ridding it of excesses and inequities. BCBSA also joined with a large HMO trade association to endorse accountable health plan standards that were shared by most of the proposals under consideration.

The BCBSNC Governmental Affairs staff spent much of its time during 1992 and 1993 studying the major reform proposals to weigh the merits and drawbacks of each. Governmental Affairs staffers diligently provided information and statistics that supported the business interests of the Plan and the health of its subscribers to those public policymakers considering reform. In 1993, the North Carolina legislature ratified several health care reform bills. The most notable of these was the Health Care Reform Act, which called for the creation of a state health care plan that would improve access to health insurance for small employers and self-employed individuals through voluntary purchasing alliances. But at the federal level, hope for significant health care reform was fading as time passed and challenges to the Clinton plan grew louder.

As Americans responded vehemently to their new president's vision of health care reform, BCBSNC began preparing for its own transition in leadership. In March 1993, Plan President

Tom Rose announced that he would retire at the end of the year. For 20 years—one-third of the company's lifetime—Rose had built BCBSNC's reputation among Blue Plans for its comparative financial stability and administrative efficiency. As he departed, Rose clearly recognized that health care reform and managed care were the key issues facing the industry at large and BCBSNC. The BCBSNC board of trustees' search for his successor focused on expertise in managing the complexity inherent in a rapidly changing health care market, acknowledging that it was time for nontraditional approaches to industry issues.

The Board chose Kenneth (Ken) C. Otis, II, who came on board as the new BCBSNC president in January 1994. Otis had been an executive at Blue Cross and Blue Shield of Florida, a state whose managed care enrollment had always led the way among both Blue Plans and commercial carriers in the Southeast. His responsibilities at the Florida Plan included all marketing, managed care, and field operations, and he had also served in executive positions with commercial insurance companies. He knew that the health care industry was in a significant state of transition from traditional, indemnity-style

products to managed care—a business model entirely different from the one in use only a few years earlier.

Otis quickly discovered that the business focus at the North Carolina Plan was very different from that of Florida. He recalled: "When I arrived, it was clear that the business was viewed as processing claims, sort of a high-volume, low-cost manufacturing operation. We needed a different paradigm in which the goal was to manage total costs, not just claims costs. We needed a bigger portfolio of managed care products. And most important, we needed to understand that we were overwhelmingly in the business of managing and delivering care."[4]

Otis brought to BCBSNC not only his experience in managed care, but a different style of leadership. Former Plan President Tom Rose had exercised a more traditional, hierarchical, top-down style of leadership. The more transactional work environment of the Rose era had been appropriate for the many years when the business was claims-focused and efficiency-driven. But Otis brought a more participative leadership style in which strategy, results, and effectiveness were central. "We set different kinds of expectations for people," Otis recalled, and

Kenneth (Ken) C. Otis, II, served as president of BCBSNC from 1994 to 2000. His transitional leadership helped the Plan embrace a new business model and develop a larger portfolio of managed care products. Photo courtesy of BCBSNC archives.

1993

In 1993, First Lady Hillary Rodham Clinton leads a failed effort to create a national plan that provides affordable health care for all Americans.

In 1993, researchers clone human embryos for the first time, provoking a storm of ethical protest.

In the early 1990s, genetic research yields major finds: genes are located for Alzheimer's disease, breast cancer, colon cancer, hyperactivity disorder, diabetes, Lou Gehrig's disease, and Huntington's chorea.

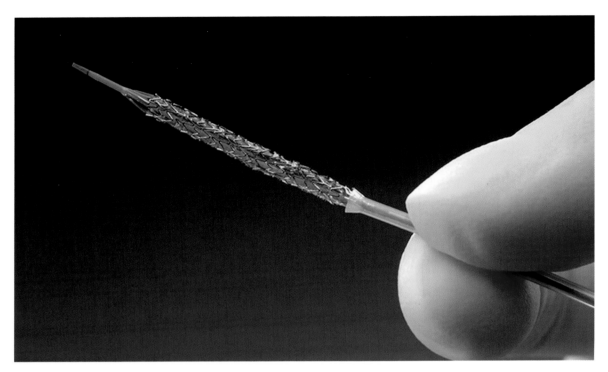

Development of the coronary artery stent in 1994 allowed the mechanical widening of blood vessels, a viable alternative to heart surgery. Photo courtesy of U.S. Food and Drug Administration.

"a lot of people didn't like the new ground rules and didn't perform as well under them."[5]

Faced not only with implementing this paradigm shift but also with the prospect of a national health care plan, Otis was quickly asked by his new staff whether he saw the Clinton plan as a threat or an opportunity for BCBSNC. His answer in late 1993, before he had even arrived in North Carolina, was prescient: "I think we are likely to get something less sweeping than as proposed. It is more likely to evolve."[6]

In fact, by September 1994, exactly one year after its introduction, the Clinton Health

Security Act was declared dead. Its defeat could be credited to many variables—the plan's complexity and budget, political power struggles, fear of too much government control, even distrust of the Clintons themselves. Whatever the ultimate cause, it certainly proved to be a major chapter in the long story of repeated attempts to enact national health insurance, each one giving way to the powerful American dedication to free market forces. As health care historian Paul Starr, who also served as a senior adviser in the formulation of the Clinton health plan, acknowledged: "We misjudged the health care politics of 1993 as a change in the climate when it was only a change in the weather."[7]

The battle over federal health care reform certainly took center stage during Ken Otis's first year as BCBSNC president. The Plan had come out clearly in favor of the principles behind the Clinton plan but squarely against the mandatory health alliances and premium caps it required. Otis recognized that there were both pros and cons inherent in the plan for federally run health care: "There is some irony in that the proposal could have been very good for Blue Plans; they would have been in a position to be the administrators for some sort of national health insurance as they had been for Medicare and other government programs. But we were so convinced that this was the wrong thing for our members and the public at large. I really was, and still am, an advocate of letting the market work and defining the role of government as policing abusers, creating a level playing field, and providing information—'steering the boat, not rowing the boat.' So I was horrified at any notion of a nationally run program."[8]

Once the Clinton plan was defeated, the private sector could proceed without distraction to the business of voluntary health care reform. The initiative for change in health systems would continue to be defined in local markets and regulatory environments, as it was in North Carolina.

Evolution or Revolution?

Despite the time and attention required by the federal health care reform debate, BCBSNC was able to continue its concerted efforts to understand and respond to the changing needs of the state market, looking for ways to increase access to health care while carefully managing costs. Plan President Otis shrewdly recognized a critical window of opportunity during which BCBSNC could further capitalize on the managed care-hungry market. Doing so would require company-wide changes and the expansion of many capabilities—from marketing to product development, from management to systems

(see *I Remember: "A revolution was about to take place . . ."*). The Plan made particularly heavy investments in its technical infrastructure, updating its 1970s-era claims processing system to serve the demands of more modern managed care information processing.

Early in Otis's tenure as president, the results were positive. Preferred Care, the Plan's preferred provider organization (PPO), made gains in enrollment and was available in nearly all of the state's 100 counties. The company also introduced a new comprehensive PPO product, Preferred Care® *Select*, which offered more flexibility in the choice of providers while reimbursing doctors on a fixed-fee schedule. Enrollment in the Plan's signature HMO, the Personal Care Plan (PCP), jumped nearly 27 percent in 1994. Six new plans were introduced within the PCP product line in 1995, driving another 49 percent gain. BCBSNC also began offering Med*Point*[SM], its first point-of-service (POS) product, which allowed members to choose a provider within the Plan's network or seek medical care outside the network. Med*Point* gained 40,000 members in a single year. By the end of 1994, BCBSNC was the leader in managed health care in the state, and plans for broadening the product spectrum

1993

1994

A new body imaging technology called functional Magnetic Resonance Imaging (fMRI) is developed in 1993. It greatly improves the ability to map the functions of various areas of the human brain.

The United States is declared a polio-free zone in 1994.

In 1994, the FDA approves two breakthroughs: the coronary artery stent and a new surgical laser procedure (keratotomy) for correcting vision problems.

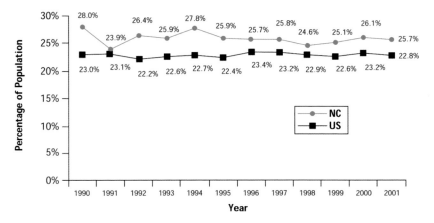

Despite repeated warnings from the FDA, smoking rates in the United States, particularly among young people, continued to pose health care challenges. In North Carolina, with its tobacco legacy, rates remained higher. Graph courtesy of BCBSNC 2003 report on the State of Preventive Health.

included the introduction of 16 new options to its PPO by 1996. Blue Advantage® became its first managed care plan designed for those not covered by employer-sponsored groups, and within only a few months, enrollment tripled the company's projections. Overall, the company's managed care plans had achieved major liftoff, helping thousands more North Carolinians to access health care they could afford.

Unexpected Turns

As the managed care revolution took place, it seemed that all of the rules in health care were changing—from financing and delivery to product marketing and provider contracting. Even the long-standing legal status of Blue Plans was changing. In a landmark 1994 decision, the

BCBSA board voted to eliminate the requirement that all member Plans maintain not-for-profit status. Even though all Blue Plans had become subject to federal income tax under the Tax Reform Act of 1986, some Plans (including BCBSNC) were still considered not-for-profit at the state level (see *Did You Know?*). Once this requirement was lifted and investor ownership was allowed, new business possibilities opened up for consideration, such as regional consolidation. Some Blue Plans quickly converted to for-profit status—Blue Cross of California in 1996, for one—to take immediate advantage of such opportunities. BCBSNC did not pursue conversion at that time, as neither Plan President Otis nor the board of trustees yet saw it to be in the company's best interest.

While the conversion option would pose both major promise and painful public scrutiny in the near future, BCBSNC faced unforeseen challenges in another business-critical area. High technology was now ubiquitous, driving greater efficiency in sharing information across every sector of the economy but also creating new and significant security risks. This was particularly true for the health insurance industry, as sensitive medical information was being transmitted widely between hospitals, outpatient clinics, physician practices, and insurers for admissions, testing, and claims processing purposes. In the late 1990s, two abbreviations—HIPAA and Y2K—would enter the vocabulary of information exchange and risk management, costing

BCBSNC millions of dollars in compliance and readiness for the new millennium.

The federal Health Insurance Portability and Accountability Act (HIPAA) passed into law in August 1996 for two major purposes: (1) to protect health insurance coverage for workers and their families when they change or lose their jobs; and (2) to provide for a uniform, basic level of security and privacy of health information throughout the country. Prior to the enactment of HIPAA, privacy rules and regulations varied from state to state and even from one health care organization to another.[11] But as Harry Reynolds, BCBSNC vice president of IS Planning and Information Compliance, noted, the issue of "portability" proved to be the easy part: "The problem is there were two simple, little words in that legislation called 'administrative simplification.' That has now turned into HIPAA privacy, HIPAA security, HIPAA transactions, and code sets through which every hospital and doctor can send a claim to every payer in the same format."[12]

HIPAA legislation, while based on good intentions, required massive, complex, and costly implementation to achieve the administrative simplification required of hospitals, medical practices, and health insurers such as BCBSNC. Only authorized personnel were allowed access to patient medical information, and HIPAA rules further stipulated that only the information necessary for a task be available to them. Reynolds acknowledged that administrative simplification created complex legalities, potential penalties,

The 1996 federal Health Insurance Portability and Accountability Act was passed to ensure the privacy of patient health information. Photo courtesy of U.S. Department of Health and Human Services.

a blizzard of additional paperwork, and untold additional staff hours: "HIPAA has driven a dramatic amount of change here. We've spent tens of millions of dollars to achieve HIPAA compliance."[13]

While the HIPAA legislation allowed companies several years to achieve compliance, many companies were slow to implement the necessary changes. First, the specific guidelines emerged piecemeal from the federal government between 1998 and 2000. In addition, there was a pervasive computer-programming problem that needed to be addressed during the same period. As the millennium year 2000 approached, there was significant concern that the changeover from the common computer program design of using a two-digit date format (e.g., 99 instead of 1999) to a four-digit format could cause a disruption or failure of critical functions in major industries. This programming concern—known as Y2K—blossomed into a national fear and staple of media speculation as January 1, 2000, approached.

The Y2K problem required companies to check and upgrade their computer systems and do major contingency planning in case the feared breakdowns took place. It was a double whammy for information technology professionals in health care as they tackled the demands of both HIPAA compliance and Y2K readiness simultaneously. At BCBSNC, these unexpected demands strained not only the technical staff and infrastructure but available financial resources as well. Bob Greczyn, then chief operating officer of BCBSNC, recognized that the Plan was somewhat handicapped in its change readiness by its not-for-profit status relative to its commercial competitors: "We could probably respond faster to an involuntary circumstance like Y2K or HIPAA if we had the ability to access the capital markets."[14]

There was little choice but to invest the human and financial resources necessary to surmount the challenges posed by the HIPAA legislative provisions and the Y2K "bug." But as Plan leaders knew all too well, there would be other unplanned demands like these in the future. Competition became particularly fierce as the 1990s progressed. The total number of HMOs in North Carolina leaped from 10 in 1993 to a peak of 24 in 1997. Both delivery and financing of the health care system was shifting and consolidating, as HMOs bought physician practices and providers formed their own organizations. In an attempt to control health care costs, "capitation" became a dominant system of financing. Capitation payments shifted the risk for medical costs to providers by paying for each customer served instead of for services performed. Insurers, patients, and payers were in deeply unfamiliar territory.

Remaining competitive in this era of unrelenting change would call for visionary leadership, a robust and innovative business strategy, superb customer responsiveness, and deep financial resources. Ready access to additional capital could occur only through loans or through developing new lines of business outside the geographic boundaries of North Carolina. The realities could be addressed by conversion to for-profit status. Although BCBSNC's history of financial stability gave the Plan significant borrowing capacity, the cost of loans would ultimately be paid by the members and was regarded as an undesirable option. Was it time to convert? For the first five years after this option was introduced, BCBSNC's answer was no. As President Ken Otis stated, "I think it's useful for the people of North Carolina to have a company whose sole business is to focus on the problems, the needs, the provider peculiarities and the delivery systems in this state—free from having to worry about being acquired and free from worrying about shareholder pressures to grow the business and bottom line on a near-term basis."[15]

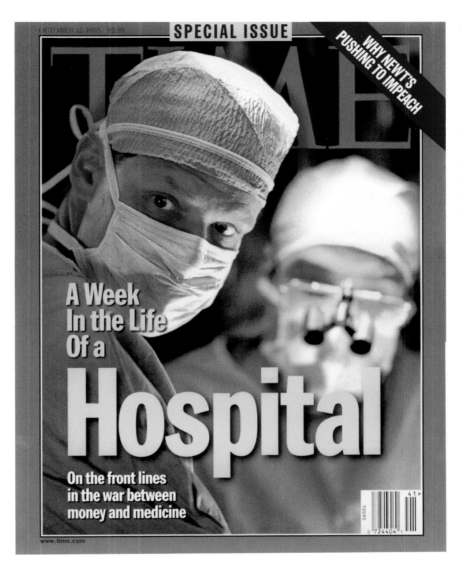

SPECIAL ISSUE

WHY NEWT'S PUSHING TO IMPEACH

OCTOBER 12 1998 $2.95

TIME

A Week In the Life Of a Hospital

On the front lines in the war between money and medicine

www.time.com

As managed care became the dominant model of health care delivery and financing in the 1990s, many hospitals and physician clinics lost money. Some merged with larger HMO companies or became part of regional health care systems in order to survive. Photo courtesy of Time Inc.

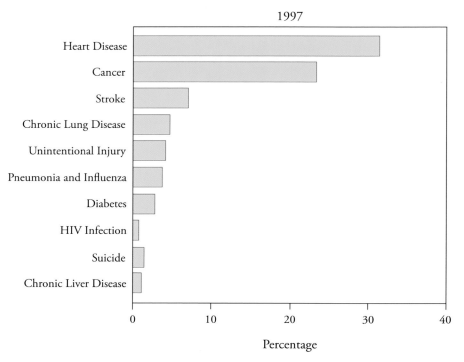

1997

Heart Disease
Cancer
Stroke
Chronic Lung Disease
Unintentional Injury
Pneumonia and Influenza
Diabetes
HIV Infection
Suicide
Chronic Liver Disease

0   10   20   30   40

Percentage

The 10 leading causes of death in the United States in 1997 as a percentage of all deaths. Medical conditions rather than infectious diseases became more prevalent over the course of the 20th century. Photo courtesy of the National Center for Health Statistics.

But in 1995 BCBSNC was forced to react, recalled BCBSNC Vice President for Governmental Affairs Brad Adcock, to a Department of Insurance draft legislative proposal on conversion, including efforts to seize the company's reserves in the event of conversion. "There was legislation," BCBSNC Adcock remembered, "that, had it passed, would have converted BCBSNC to a for-profit company and made it possible for the state to inappropriately seize company assets from our policyholders."[16]

BCBSNC's Governmental Affairs staff quickly assessed the situation and worked to

determine the legislation's specific intent. "We analyzed the proposed legislation and brought legal counsel on board to more carefully review the bill's language and its implications for the Plan should the bill be enacted," said Adcock.[17] Ultimately, BCBSNC was able to propose language for inclusion in the bill that would both make it consumer-friendly and enable BCBSNC to remain financially viable if it ever decided to pursue conversion.

The state's General Assembly emerged with its first proposal in the spring of 1997. The intent to further "level the playing field" between not-for-profit companies in the health care industry and their for-profit competitors was clear: "The General Assembly recognizes the substantial and recent changes in market and health care conditions that are affecting these corporations and the benefit of equal regulatory treatment and competitive equality for health care insurers. . . . A procedure for conversion is in the best interest of policyholders because it will provide greater financial stability for these corporations and a greater opportunity for the corporations to remain financially independent."[18]

While BCBSNC certainly favored the concept of equal regulatory treatment, it felt that some of the specific provisions embedded in the legislation required deeper study and definition. For example, conversion would require that

- the fair market value of the company be placed in a tax-exempt charitable foundation to promote the health care of the people in the state

- no employee, director, or officer benefit directly from conversion
- the conversion plan be in the public interest and fair to current policyholders
- a forecast of premium rates for three years following conversion be developed
- a period of public comment and public access to records related to the conversion be part of the process
- both the state Insurance Commissioner and state Attorney General have the right to review and power to approve any conversion plan filed.[19]

What did "public interest" really mean? Did the assets of BCBSNC belong to the policyholders or to the public? As Adcock asserted, "Politically speaking, for many years the regulatory agencies, elected officials, and most everyone else had agreed that policyholders were the owners. That was also the initial interpretation firmly put forward by legal analysts, so the legislation was written that way. Yet to our credit, we also placed language in it stating that the Attorney General had the power to have the courts decide this issue

if he wanted to."[20] The terms of the conversion legislation began to be hotly debated not only by BCBSNC but by regulators and consumer advocates as well. By the summer of 1997, the legislature referred the legislation to a study commission and issued a moratorium on conversion filings.[21] The final legislation emerged in the form of three 1998 statutes and ultimately clarified the fact that BCBSNC assets did not belong to the policyholders. But the real drama would ensue only when a conversion plan was filed and subjected to the approval process. Although the Plan was not yet interested in pursuing the conversion option, the Governmental Affairs staff had become immersed in the development of the legislation as a strategic part of its efforts to influence industry and regulatory trends.

Entering the Age of Information— An Age of Choice

While the HMO market in the late 1980s had experienced a widespread bust in which many went bankrupt, the 1990s were a period of impressive recovery for the survivors. Nationally, total HMO enrollment increased from 39 million in 1992 to 79 million in 1998. BCBSNC's

In 1998 BCBSNC launched both internal and external Web sites. Members could now find providers, products, and health information online. Photo courtesy of BCBSNC archives.

1995

In 1995, the first osteoporosis drug not made from hormones is introduced.

The link between human papillomavirus (HPV) and development of cervical cancer is found in 1995.

Despite 30 years of warnings about tobacco use, the nation persists in smoking, and North Carolina fares even worse. Lung cancer rates tell a gruesome story, rising by 1,500 percent between 1930 and 1990.

I Remember: "These HMOs came and went . . ."

Dr. Don Bradley, current executive medical director for BCBSNC, recalled the period in which the popularity of HMOs soared and then dramatically faltered. In one of its many efforts to adapt to the changing health care system, BCBSNC learned a hard lesson: "This was a time in the 1990s when a number of health plans and hospital providers thought vertical integration was the way to go. Hospitals tried to become insurance companies, so they bought practices. Insurance companies thought they would become providers, so they tried to buy practices. We spent a lot of money buying primary care practices, and it just didn't yield a good return on our investment. A number of doctors whose practices were purchased at really premium prices said, 'I'm now a salaried employee, and I'll just come to work and do my thing,' and they lost interest in trying to manage the overall care. So the insurance plans and hospitals that had purchased these practices just couldn't get a business return on investment, and they found that to be a real problem.

That's another place where the whole health care system really got into a pickle. We, the insurance companies, are not providers. We don't really know how to deliver care at the patient level, and we shouldn't be doing that. Providers are terrible insurance companies, and they shouldn't be trying to provide insurance products. I think that's why a lot of these HMOs came and went."[22]

Valerie Carter, director of Corporate Planning for BCBSNC, also vividly recalls a turning point in public perception of HMOs during that period: "I can remember the absolute moment when I knew something was going awry. I didn't see the backlash coming until I saw the 1997 movie *As Good as It Gets,* with Jack Nicholson and Helen Hunt. The whole audience cheered aloud when one of the characters swore about an HMO's ineffective treatment of her asthmatic son! I remember coming into one of our strategy team meetings and saying, 'Have you seen the movie? Have you heard the audience?'"[23]

HMO, the Personal Care Plan, nearly tripled its enrollment during Otis's tenure, growing from 82,000 members in 1994 to nearly a quarter million in 1999. Yet the growing numbers of HMO members—in North Carolina and across the nation—also came to resent the inherent restrictions of the gatekeeper model, and a pervasive hostility toward HMOs broke out among health care consumers (see *I Remember: "These HMOs came and went . . ."*).

Member surveys and provider feedback strongly indicated that BCBSNC needed to simplify the process and allow HMO members to change physicians by simply making a phone call. Ken Lerner, vice president of Marketing and Saegis Benefits[SM], Inc., a BCBSNC subsidiary, recalled: "We listened to the market, and by the end of the 1990s, we decided to develop our HMO products without gatekeepers. We were one of the first companies in North Carolina to make that shift."[24] It was clear that patients wanted a greater choice of physicians and hospitals, more active participation in their medical decisions, and access to clear information. These and other consumer needs were captured in the Consumer Bill of Rights and Responsibilities, a blueprint developed by the Clinton administra-

In 1995, the FDA declares cigarettes to be "drug delivery devices." Restrictions are proposed on marketing and sales to reduce smoking by young people.

In 1996, scientists study a new type of pain and anti-inflammatory medication—the COX-2 inhibitor.

In 1997, the World Health Organization (WHO) reports a severe obesity epidemic throughout much of the world, affecting adults and children alike.

tion that outlined specific principles of consumer protection and quality health care.[25] BCBSNC became one of the first insurers in the nation to voluntarily adopt these safeguards for health care consumers in 1998.

With the marked trend away from HMOs and toward the greater flexibility of PPOs, BCBSNC began developing product lines with significantly more managed care options (see *A Sign of the Times*). The Plan was also increasingly emphasizing prevention and wellness. Many products included preventive benefits, such as immunizations, annual physical exams, and routine screenings. Some types of coverage moved beyond the limits of traditional medicine. For example, a discount program for alternative medicine services, such as acupuncture, yoga, and biofeedback, was introduced in 1999. Another discount program provided savings for seniors on out-of-pocket expenses for prescriptions, hearing aids, and vision care. The Plan also expanded its business by entering a five-year subcontract with Anthem Alliance for Health to service TriCare (CHAMPUS), gaining a half million members from 21 service centers in North Carolina and Virginia.

BCBSNC was not only changing what it was selling but how it was selling its products. With the advent of the Internet as a primary source of information, the explosion of consumers buying goods and services online transformed the Plan's communication and sales and marketing strategies. In 1998, BCBSNC launched both internal

The Consumer Bill of Rights and Responsibilities

Blue Cross and Blue Shield of North Carolina proudly endorses the following principles as part of its commitment to providing quality, affordable health care to North Carolinians.

We believe that:

- North Carolinians have the right to receive accurate, easily understood information to help them make informed decisions about their health care.

- North Carolinians have the right to choose physicians and hospitals that offer high-quality care.

- North Carolinians have the right to seek emergency health care when needed.

- North Carolinians have the right and responsibility to participate actively in all decisions related to their health care.

- North Carolinians have the right to considerate, respectful care from health plans and from all health professionals—at all times and under all circumstances.

- North Carolinians have the right to confidentiality in their communications with physicians and hospitals. North Carolinians also have the right to review, copy and request amendments to their medical records.

- North Carolinians have the right to a fair and efficient process for resolving differences with their health plans, physicians and hospitals.

We encourage all North Carolinians to become more involved in their own health and well-being. These recommendations were developed by the bipartisan President's Advisory Commission on Consumer Protection and Quality in the Health Care Industry.

Blue Cross and Blue Shield of North Carolina formally endorsed the Consumer Bill of Rights and Responsibilities on October 8, 1998, becoming the first health plan in North Carolina, and one of the first in the nation, to announce its intention to voluntarily comply with this bill of rights.

Blue Cross and Blue Shield of North Carolina is an independent licensee of the Blue Cross and Blue Shield Association.

The Consumer Bill of Rights and Responsibilities developed by the Clinton administration outlined specific principles of consumer protection and quality health care. BCBSNC became one of the first insurers in the nation to voluntarily adopt these safeguards for health care consumers in 1998. Photo courtesy of BCBSNC archives.

BCBSNC sponsored the Caring Program for Children for more than a decade, providing free health coverage to some 30,000 children whose parents did not qualify for Medicaid but could not afford to purchase health insurance. Photo courtesy of BCBSNC archives.

and external Web sites. Members could now find providers and specialists in their area and access information about products and wellness online. By the following year, the Plan was fully engaged in e-commerce, providing prospective members with instant rate quotes after they answered a quick online survey about their health and insurance needs. Growth in membership, products, and services also precipitated the need for more staff and more space. Construction on a new 220,000-square-foot Customer Service Center building in Durham began in 1997, and the new Customer Service Center was dedicated in 1998. Bringing most operational areas under one roof would create an environment more conducive to results-oriented teamwork and more efficient workflows. A strong group of new senior executives came on board as well. BCBSNC was expanding its capabilities and, in so doing, its reach.

A Partner in Community Health

Since the company's founding in 1933, its mission had been to promote the greater health of all North Carolinians. Sixty years later BCBSNC was fulfilling that mission not only through its

products but also through community health programs, corporate sponsorships, and donations. This commitment continued throughout the 1990s, often demonstrated in programs focused on children's health. Four-term North Carolina Governor James B. (Jim) Hunt, Jr., recognized the Plan's support of the state's early childhood initiative known as Smart Start: "I remember when we started Smart Start in 1993 Blue Cross and Blue Shield of North Carolina understood the importance of every child in this state starting to school healthy and ready to learn."[26] The company had also underwritten the Caring Program for Children[SM] for more than a decade, providing free health coverage to some 30,000 children whose parents did not qualify for Medicaid but could not afford to purchase health insurance. In partnership with the state's top leaders and health and fitness advocates, BCBSNC launched Be Active Kids[SM], an interactive nutrition and physical fitness program for preschool children, in 1999.

As BCBSNC moved toward the first decade of the new millennium, it would continue to help its customers and communities statewide improve their health. Although the company sustained operating losses of $200 million between 1995

Cardiovascular disease, cancer, and stroke remain the leading causes of death in the United States.

A routine blood test, the prostate-specific antigen test (PSA), is introduced in 1998 to improve diagnosis of prostate cancer.

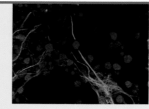

In 1998, embryonic stem cells, which give rise to every kind of human tissue, are grown in a Petri dish. The discovery is hailed as a landmark event with vast biomedical potential but also raises daunting legal and ethical concerns.

and 1999, it was also building business-critical infrastructure and capabilities during that period. The company had faced a difficult convergence of events during the late 1990s—the emergence of HIPAA and for-profit conversion legislation, the technology demands of Y2K, a rapidly changing managed care market, and a major transition in leadership and direction. As Plan president, Ken Otis had initiated across-the-board, business-critical changes that he acknowledged were painful: "I see my tenure as transitional. It was wrenching to see the stresses on the marketplace, what was going on with the insurance department and the providers, and how the changes affected the people in the organization. I started and took us a fair way through the transition to being an effective competitor in the marketplace with good, strong managed care capabilities as well as a better traditional insurance company.

When I left, things were going in the right direction, and a lot of that due to having brought on people like Bob Greczyn. But we were still very fragile when I left."[27]

Just as the company was stabilizing, Otis announced that he would retire in April 2000. Robert J. (Bob) Greczyn, Jr., who had been serving as chief operating officer since 1998, was quickly named the next president and chief executive officer. Greczyn faced a tremendous opportunity to build on the Plan's legacy while charting new territories in business development. But he would do so as BCBSNC attempted to secure a stronghold in the most competitive, cost-pressured health care market in history. The Plan would need to bring twenty-first-century technology, innovation, and keen business strategy to its age-old mission of improving the health of all North Carolinians.

In response to a growing epidemic of obesity among children, BCBSNC launched Be Active Kids®, an interactive nutrition and physical fitness program for preschool children, in 1999. Be Active Kids would eventually become a signature program of the BCBSNC Foundation. Photo courtesy of BCBSNC archives.

Viagra, the first pill for erectile dysfunction, enters and storms the drug market in 1998.

In 1998, the first vaccine for Lyme disease is developed.

The Clinton administration endorses the Consumer Bill of Rights, which outlines principles of consumer protection and quality health care. BCBSNC becomes one of the first insurers in the nation to voluntarily adopt them in 1998.

The West Nile virus first appears in the United States in 1999.

Chapter Eight

A New Blue for the New Millennium

Turnaround

As the clock ticked past midnight and the new millennium officially arrived on January 1, 2000, information technology professionals around the globe began celebrating a welcome non-event: nothing happened. The widespread failure of computer applications and infrastructure expected to result from the Y2K problem did not materialize. Although $300 billion had been spent nationally (over $40 million by BCBSNC alone) during the late 1990s for Y2K readiness, it remains unclear whether it had been an overpublicized hoax or a case study in averted catastrophe.[1] Regardless, BCBSNC entered the decade unencumbered by serious worries about systems performance.

However, there were other well-founded worries to address. In North Carolina, the economy and population had changed dramatically over the past several decades. The once-vital textile industry had significantly downsized in the face of global competition, and tobacco was far from king, destabilizing the state's revenue streams and contributing to a growing number of uninsured. Health care expenditures had continued to rise to new heights, representing 13.8 percent of the national gross domestic product in 2000. Competition for the growing managed care market remained intense, driving the need for rapid, innovative new product development and intense marketing campaigns. The company's financial performance had been disappointing for several years, with sustained operating losses in the millions. And BCBSNC President Ken Otis was retiring after only six years, setting another leadership transition in motion. What the Plan needed now was a turnaround leader who could help find new ways to address access and affordability in the state.

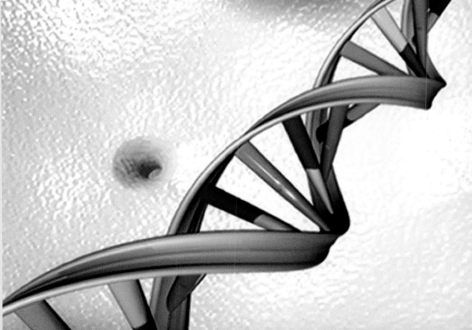

In 2000 scientists succeeded in mapping the human genome, opening up countless new applications in medicine and many other fields. Photo courtesy of the National Human Genome Research Institute.

Robert (Bob) J. Greczyn, Jr., joined BCBSNC as chief operating officer in 1998 and by 2000 was named president and CEO. Photo courtesy of BCBSNC archives.

With that in mind, the Board identified a promising successor. In 1999, Robert (Bob) J. Greczyn, Jr., became BCBSNC's new president, and in 2000, chief executive officer as well. Greczyn had come to the Plan as chief operating officer in 1998, bringing substantial experience in the health care insurance industry. Fifteen years earlier, he had worked in professional relations for Health America Corporation of North Carolina, one of the state's original HMOs. From there, he had a series of roles with Principal Health Care of Delaware, returned to North Carolina and built the state's largest HMO (Healthsource Health Plans), and then went to CIGNA HealthCare. But Greczyn also brought a critical public health lens to his role. He had earned a master's degree in public health from UNC–Chapel Hill and had built and run a community health center in rural Anson County, North Carolina.[2] Greczyn deeply understood the trend toward managed care, the competition, and customer health issues, all of which would help him create a well-grounded new vision for BCBSNC in the state's shifting health care market.

Whereas Plan President Ken Otis had begun the movement toward a diverse portfolio of managed care products, Bob Greczyn would be the leader to articulate a new mission and identity for BCBSNC as a health care company, an advocate for preventive health care, and a provider of information for making healthy lifestyle choices. The new mission implied a whole new way of doing business, one in which customer focus was a key priority and central to the turnaround strategy. In 2000 the company proclaimed a new customer promise, distilled to the core message: "Simplify. Assist. Empower." As Greczyn explained:

> "One of the first things we did was introduce the fact that the customer is essential to everything we do. I think that was a change for Blue Cross and Blue Shield of North Carolina. We began to focus on the importance of the customer, the importance of the products, services, and information we can provide them, and the impact that we can have on their ability to improve their own health."[3]

Brand New

To communicate its new mission, the company developed a compelling, multidimensional marketing campaign to reach out to its customers. User-friendly online information,

In 2000, the average life expectancy in the United States is 77 years. In North Carolina, it is 75.8 years, ranking the state 40th in the nation.

A new 3-D computer imaging process (virtual colonoscopy) developed in 2000 allows doctors to observe intestines painlessly and to screen for colon cancer.

television advertising, and brand recognition were all critical to raising customer awareness of BCBSNC's products, services, and information. The company capitalized on the fact that the Blues had the number one health care brand in the country and launched an entire suite of new products in 2000, all tied to the Blue name. In addition to its managed care options, the Plan now offered an affordable dental plan, comprehensive medical information service, and healthy lifestyle programs.

Of course, this suite of new products was driven by careful market research on the needs of the Plan's various customer segments. Research indicated that customers wanted more choice and flexibility along with easier access to physicians and specialists. By meeting these needs through effectively marketed product features, the company's turnaround strategy soon yielded positive results in 2000, as BCBSNC experienced its first profits since 1994. Its preferred provider organizations continued to make significant gains, approaching the benchmark of 1 million members that year. Overall membership grew by 15 percent and the large national account business by an astonishing 60 percent. The new millennium dawned full of promise.

To help anchor the company's transition, Greczyn also worked with his new senior leadership team and employees to create a set of guiding principles that captured the company's purpose and core values. One of those principles—"seek to make a difference in our communities"—came to life in late 2000 in the form of the Blue Cross and Blue Shield of North Carolina Foundation. The Foundation was created as a separate, independent, private, charitable foundation aimed at improving the health and well-being of North Carolinians. As Kathy Higgins, BCBSNC Foundation president and vice president of Community Relations for BCBSNC, recalled: "Bob helped us take our community relations focus to a much higher level. He challenged us to think about how we could impact people's lives in a way that is really meaningful and has measurable outcomes. And we saw that we could make an even greater difference if we didn't depend on our business cycle."[4] With an initial investment of $15 million, the Foundation could reliably offer programs and grants to communities even if the company's bottom line fluctuated.

The BCBSNC Foundation was established in 2000 and is dedicated to improving the health of vulnerable populations, encouraging healthy, active communities, and increasing the effectiveness of nonprofit organizations. Photo courtesy of BCBSNC Foundation.

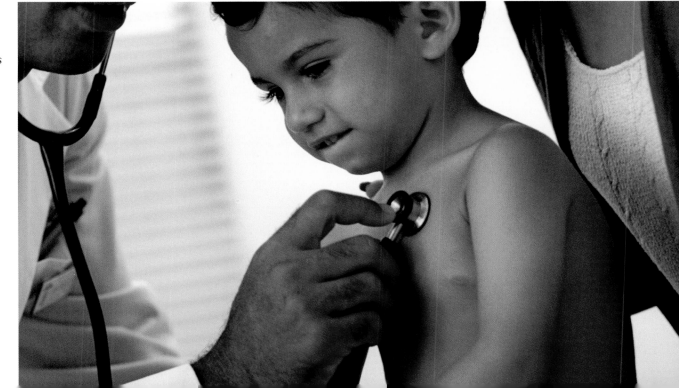

The Foundation began with a few key focus areas: meeting the needs of the uninsured; eliminating racial and ethnic health disparities; and promoting screenings, education, and physical activity. As Higgins pointed out: "We wanted to make a difference in health education by creating signature programs. We knew we could do that not only through financial means, but also through bringing our internal expertise to the table and working with nonprofit organizations to solve problems."[5] For example, in recognition of the state's growing obesity problem, the Foundation managed and supported the Be Active Kids program, a physical activity and nutrition program for four- and five-year-olds. The Foundation also wanted to help strengthen organizational capabilities within nonprofit groups, so it began offering regional training workshops through its Healthy Community Institute for Nonprofit Excellence.

The Foundation also offered a grant program —typically in amounts up to $25,000—for nonprofit organizations whose initiatives were aligned with its focus areas. The first grants were awarded in 2000, led by $1 million to aid the uninsured of eastern North Carolina. By working to improve the health outcomes of the state's most vulnerable populations, the BCBSNC Foundation was indeed making a difference.

Leadership Transitions

The first year under Bob Greczyn's new leadership effected a real turnaround for BCBSNC. But it was a time of significant leadership transition at the state and national levels as well. In 2000 longtime Democratic Governor James (Jim) B. Hunt, Jr., was finishing the second of two consecutive terms in office, during which he helped to nurture tremendous economic growth in the state while undertaking serious educational reforms. Hunt had long valued BCBSNC's role as "the state's insurer" and its commitment to health care: "I can tell you that from the very beginning Blue Cross and Blue Shield of North Carolina has been concerned about more than just the people in high-tech areas of the state where people can afford insurance better than other places. They've not only covered the state as an insurance company but they have worked with the state to try to make sure that we have good health care from the beginning of life on for all of our people."[6] Hunt was succeeded by Democratic Governor Mike Easley, former state

A powerful new blood clot–busting drug reduces treatment time for heart attack victims from 90 minutes to 5 seconds.

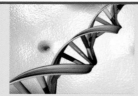

In 2000, in a landmark event of genetic research, scientists succeed in mapping the human genome—the sequence of all genetic pairs in human DNA.

Published in 2001, the "Nun Study" sheds light on the nature and development of Alzheimer's disease.

Attorney General, who continued to support education reform and champion improved access to health care for North Carolina's underinsured.

Two-term Democratic President Bill Clinton was also leaving office amid one of the most hotly contested presidential elections in U.S. history. Although the idea of universal health care had derailed during the Clinton administration, candidates Al Gore and George W. Bush still campaigned heavily on health care issues. Prescription drug coverage for seniors and Medicare solvency became central points of debate. Democrat Gore directly challenged the pharmaceutical companies and HMOs, who heavily favored Bush's Republican platform, to reform some of their consumer practices. But once the election was finalized—only after disputed vote counts in Florida were resolved by a U.S. Supreme Court decision—the presidency went to George W. Bush.

Ultimately, a new president at the national level and a new governor at the state level did not produce major changes in the direction of health care in North Carolina. The free market approach prevailed in the hope that managed care could moderate soaring health care costs. The number of Americans without health insurance continued to climb, including over a million North Carolinians, while employer-provided health insurance was declining.[7] It was a precarious trend for all: the public, the providers, and the payers.

Expansion

With bold new leadership and promising financial performance, BCBSNC set out to implement a growth strategy that would secure its place as the state's leading health insurer and better address the state's health care disparities. Like many growing Blue Plans across the country, BCBSNC began to consider in-state acquisitions as a means of expansion. In June 2001, the company announced that it would buy PARTNERS National Health Plans of North Carolina, Inc., the state's largest HMO, based in Winston-Salem. The largest acquisition in BCBSNC history, the deal was completed in October, bringing an additional 300,000 members on board. The acquisition included ACS Benefit Services, Inc., a provider of third-

In 2001 BCBSNC bought PARTNERS, the state's largest HMO, based in Winston-Salem. It was the Plan's largest acquisition ever, a sign of the consolidating health care system in the state and nation. Photo courtesy of BCBSNC archives.

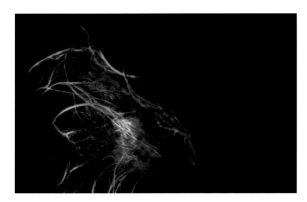

Photodynamic therapy using fiber-optic light became a promising new procedure for treating cancer, the second-leading cause of death in the United States. Photo courtesy of the Cancer Media Centre.

party administrative services for self-insured employers. Numerous synergies were realized through combining the sales forces, physician credentialing, and network contracting functions of the two organizations. The merger resulted in a stronger product mix.

The record enrollment that stemmed from the PARTNERS acquisition, coupled with the success of the new suite of products, fueled an optimism and determination to dominate the state's marketplace amid aggressive competition from national carriers. Paradoxically, it was at this moment of great strength that BCBSNC fully recognized its vulnerability as a nonprofit limited to the state's geographic boundaries. Without access to additional market capital, it would be difficult—perhaps impossible—to fund customer service and technology improvements through member premiums alone. In order to achieve significant growth, innovation, and greater customer satisfaction, the Plan needed to be able to consider not only in-state acquisitions such as PARTNERS but possible mergers and acquisitions on a regional basis as well. In a landmark change of direction driven by business necessity and the desire to bring millions in health care resources to North Carolina citizens,

BCBSNC decided that converting to for-profit status at this point made good business sense.

In December 2001, BCBSNC announced its intention to convert; the company filed the required conversion plan with state regulators on January 2, 2002. If approved, conversion would allow the company more flexibility and access to capital markets. It would also create one of the state's largest foundations, which would be dedicated solely to addressing North Carolina's health care needs. Once the conversion plan was filed, state regulators were charged with weighing the costs and benefits for consumers and exploring the proposal's legal complexities. Although BCBSNC and the North Carolina Department of Insurance had spent significant time and energy in the late 1990s creating the legislation governing conversion efforts, it would be another matter to bring the company's actual plan before intense public scrutiny.

Initially, confusion surfaced about the intention, funding, and governance of the already existing BCBSNC Foundation and the Health Foundation for North Carolina, Inc., which would be created as a result of conversion. The charitable purpose of the latter would be "to promote the health of the people of North Carolina."[8] But wasn't the BCBSNC Foundation already serving that purpose? Had it been created in anticipation of the conversion filing? Kathy Higgins, BCBSNC Foundation president, clarified: "In order to convert, the value of the assets of the company would be given to a foundation that would be created and directed by an independent board of directors for health-related purposes in North Carolina. The BCBSNC Foundation is a private foundation of the company, not to be confused with the proposed conversion foundation, and would have been totally separate from that."[9]

While Plan employees operated the BCBSNC Foundation, state Attorney General Roy Cooper would have appointed the board of the conversion foundation. The benefits of the conversion were apparent, as Cooper acknowledged upon hearing of BCBSNC's filing: "As health care costs rise and access to good care becomes more difficult, this foundation gives us a great opportunity to improve people's lives in North Carolina."[10]

But concerns about the conversion also drew significant media coverage and public concern, fueled in part by organized opposition to the proposed change to for-profit status. A small number of public interest groups and political consultants painted BCBSNC's conversion effort as one that would create higher premiums for its customers and higher salaries for its executives while restricting access to coverage for the underinsured.[11] On the heels of BCBSNC's filing, the North Carolina Department of Insurance issued a new set of conditions required for the conversion to address these concerns, while BCBSNC contended that the conditions created a built-in barrier to a competitive playing field. It was only the beginning of the company's efforts to negotiate conversion agreements with its regulators.

For 18 intense months, the media reported claims and counterclaims swirling among BCBSNC, state regulators, and consumer advocates about the intentions and likely outcomes of conversion. In the wake of heightened public sensitivity to corporate scandals such as Enron, fighting the negative public perceptions became too costly a war. Brad Wilson, chief operating officer, acknowledged: "The cost of conversion was exceeding $1 million a month, so we didn't feel it was in our customers' best interest for us to continue to make that investment when there was no reasonable likelihood of approval. We couldn't see the light at the end of the tunnel."[12]

In 2001, the implantable pump called the LVAD (left ventricular assist device) buys precious time for seriously ill heart patients waiting for a donor.

Studies show that the omega-3 fatty acids found in many fish can prevent heart disease and stroke.

By 2003, two-thirds of U.S. deaths each year can be attributed to just five chronic diseases—heart disease, cancer, stroke, chronic obstructive pulmonary disease, and diabetes.

In July 2003, Bob Greczyn announced that BCBSNC was withdrawing its plans to convert to a for-profit company.

Despite industry studies showing that conversions by other Blue Plans had had no negative effects on accessibility or affordability for consumers, fear had prevailed over actual data. Adding insult to injury, the anti-conversion forces portrayed the withdrawal as a consumer victory. But Greczyn never wavered in his attitude about the conversion effort: "I'm proud of the decision to begin the conversion, and I'm equally proud of the decision to end the conversion. Both were good decisions that were fully supported by the board of trustees of our company."[13] Yet with any significant change in direction, there was also a sense of loss and a period of uncertainty that followed among those who had believed in the vision and invested their energy in the effort.

Moving Ahead

In the wake of the conversion withdrawal decision, it was time for BCBSNC leaders to reflect, retool the business strategy, and redirect employees on how to move forward. Of course, the conversion effort was only one of many business initiatives BCBSNC had undertaken in 2002 and 2003. The company had continued to introduce new products and services to meet the fast-changing health insurance market. The long journey toward HIPAA compliance reached its zenith in 2002 as new technology and procedures were fully implemented. Improvements in service measures such as administrative efficiency enabled the company to significantly reduce its operating expense ratio. There was a surprising decline in medical costs, in part because some prescription drugs became available in generic or over-the-counter forms, which contributed to a marked reduction in medical costs. Despite the resources drained by the conversion effort, the company's financial performance in 2003 was exceptional.

In addition to being the insurer of choice, BCBSNC also sought to become North Carolina's employer of choice. As of 2005, the Plan had more than 4,000 employees. This was no longer a company populated with a largely operational staff that processed claims, but one in which employees needed to engage their critical thinking in areas from research to data analysis, from contract negotiation to customer satisfaction. Requiring a more performance-driven

2003

A promising new cancer procedure uses fiber-optic light (photodynamic therapy) to kill cancer cells without harming normal cells nearby.

Obesity continues to increase at a frightening rate: 55 percent of women in the United States are considered overweight, and 35 percent obese. As many as one in seven children are obese.

2004

By 2004, the obesity epidemic in North Carolina approaches 25 percent of the state's population. BCBSNC becomes the first insurer in the nation to offer coverage for physician visits aimed solely at solving a patient's weight problem.

culture than ever, the company strengthened its opportunities to attract, retain, and develop employees through competitive compensation, rewards programs, advanced education at Blue University, and work/life balance options. In addition, Greczyn highlighted the importance of workforce diversity by adding it to the Plan's guiding principles. He also created and served on a diversity council along with employees from all over the company. Greczyn knew that the Plan was making a real commitment to its future and bringing value to the business by embracing diversity.

As BCBSNC reinvigorated its strategic planning, clarity about how to thrive as a single-state insurer took hold. Greczyn explained: "We concluded that affordability is our number one challenge, that health care is just too expensive, and the way we feel we can tackle the cost of health care is to really focus on improving the health of our members."[14] The concept was simple but could have profound impact on health care costs. As former board chairman Rhone Sasser explained: "We know today that it is less expensive to keep someone healthy than it is to treat them after they have gotten sick. So we're going to continue to try to have individuals

In 2004 BCBSNC launched the Healthy Lifestyle Choices program to help members achieve a healthier weight and engage in lifestyle changes that can avoid serious—and costly—health problems. Photo courtesy of BCBSNC archives.

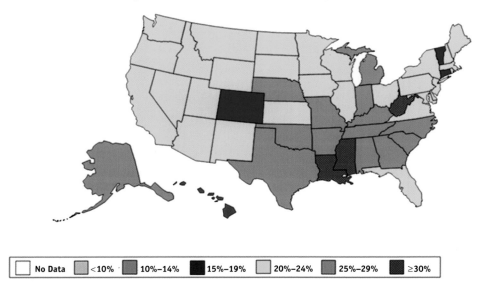

Obesity Trends* Among U.S. Adults
BRFSS, 2005
(*BMI ≥30, or ~ 30 lbs overweight for 5' 4" person)

No Data · <10% · 10%–14% · 15%–19% · 20%–24% · 25%–29% · ≥30%

In North Carolina—land of barbecued pork and banana pudding—the obesity epidemic overtook more than 25 percent of the population during the early 2000s. BCBSNC was one of the first insurers to offer coverage for physician visits aimed solely at solving a patient's weight problem. Photo courtesy of the Centers for Disease Control and Prevention.

take personal responsibility for their health care."[15]

With that focus in mind, the company rolled out an array of health management programs that provided services and education for members with any of 23 specific conditions, including chronic ones such as asthma and diabetes. A stunning 2004 report revealed that about half of BCBSNC members were considered overweight or obese, leading to the development of a new program called Healthy Lifestyle Choices. Hailed as a national model, the program provided an array of tools and services designed to help people reach and maintain a healthy weight. In 2005, BCBSNC became the first insurer in the nation to classify obesity as a "primary condition" and to offer coverage for physician visits aimed solely at solving a patient's weight problem.[16] Nurses were also available around the clock to members and to employees through on-site health screenings. In a well-crafted advertising campaign, personal testimonials underscored BCBSNC's role in providing information to help people make healthy lifestyle changes.

In addition to affordability, access to health insurance remained an issue in North Carolina, as it had since the company's beginnings. The global economy was having both positive and negative effects on the state's revenue streams and workforce. Jobs were increasingly being outsourced to nations that could provide cheaper labor. Indeed, the entire nation heard vivid stories about the plight of laid-off North Carolina textile factory workers through the 2004 election campaign of Democratic vice presidential candidate John Edwards.

The influx of Hispanic workers and families was also swelling the ranks of those needing access to low-cost or free health care. In fact, by 2005 North Carolina had one of the fastest-growing uninsured populations in the country: nearly 25 percent of those under age 65 were without coverage.[17] The percentages for racial and ethnic minorities were even higher. As a result, in the few years following its inception, the BCBSNC Foundation made numerous investments to address the profound needs of those with limited or no access to health care. In 2004, the Foundation entered into a five-year, $10 million partnership with the North Carolina Association of Free Clinics. The goal of the grant was to provide ongoing support for existing clinics and increase the number of free clinics available across the state (see *Did You Know?*).

The Foundation was also helping to provide people in rural and other medically underserved parts of North Carolina access to primary care through a five-year $10 million grant to support the Community Practitioner Program, which drew primary care doctors and other providers to underserved communities by helping to pay off their medical school loans. The North Carolina Medical Society Foundation, which manages the program, worked to raise another $5 million in matching funds.[20]

Each of these multiyear, multi-million-

Did You Know?

Through the partnership of the North Carolina Association of Free Clinics (NCAFC) and the BCBSNC Foundation, the number of free clinics available to provide quality health care to the uninsured and other vulnerable populations in the state is rapidly growing. Since the partnership began in 2004, 15 new clinics have opened, resulting in a total of 71 statewide as of 2006. The goal is to sustain the services of existing clinics and to expand the total number of free clinics and pharmacies across the state to 85, up from 56 in 2004, which will more than double the number of people served annually.

Everett Cline (shown here) suffered a heart attack, lost his job, and had no insurance. He received medical care and prescriptions at one of the many free clinics developed through the partnership of the NCAFC and BCBSNC. Photo courtesy of NCAFC.

But the numbers don't tell the whole story. The people who receive care at the free clinics do.

Consider, for example, the story of Everett Cline. After suffering a heart attack and developing rheumatoid arthritis, Cline was forced to leave his job and file for disability. He had no health insurance. Today, Cline receives care at the Davidson Medical Ministries Clinic, where he is on a long-term treatment plan and receives his eight prescriptions a month from the pharmacy. Cline is convinced that "if I hadn't been able to come here, I wouldn't be alive today."[18]

Mike Darrow, executive director of NCAFC, knew of thousands of success stories like Cline's, which added up to a real difference in the overall health of North Carolina. "The net effect of this partnership may never be truly calculated, since patients are able to return to work, remain effective in their jobs, continue to take care of their families and contribute to their local communities, thus producing a ripple effect throughout entire counties."[19]

dollar partnerships aligned strongly with the Foundation's focus areas, which were reassessed and strengthened in 2006 to increase the impact of investments on North Carolina communities. The resulting three focus areas were specifically designed to address the health of vulnerable populations, increase physical activity and healthy eating opportunities, and increase the effectiveness of nonprofit organizations.

Drawing on the company's financial strength, the BCBSNC Foundation continued to grow. In the six years since its inception, the Foundation's assets grew to $92 million, with more than $30 million in grants awarded to nonprofit organizations throughout the state. This growth gave the Foundation the flexibility to respond to the ever-changing needs of North Carolinians. For example, through donations to relief funds and volunteer support, BCBSNC had previously assisted communities devastated by the hurricanes that frequently hit the state. But the incalculable damage along the Gulf Coast resulting from Hurricane Katrina in 2005 prompted the BCBSNC Foundation to begin building a stronger emergency response infrastructure for North Carolina. By creating the Emergency Preparedness Grant Program, the Foundation provided funding to nonprofit organizations and government entities seeking to improve emergency preparedness plans and activities for vulnerable populations throughout the state.

BCBSNC continued to invest in the future health of North Carolinians in myriad ways. Customers were able to go online to buy health insurance or access information about their current coverage, research health and wellness topics, locate providers, even win prizes for being physically active. BCBSNC waived the copayment for generic prescriptions in 2006, saving customers at least $80 million. The company also provided flu vaccines to North Carolinians through statewide flu shot clinics. In addition, its partnerships with health care professionals underlined the company's commitment to helping improve health outcomes. In 2005, the company identified procedures, such as obesity surgery, that could be benchmarked and measured for high-quality results. It then designated several Centers for Excellence that could provide these procedures and monitor outcomes. Registered and licensed dietitians were added to the provider network to provide nutritional counseling to members with a desire to eat healthier. The company also collaborated with physicians, hospitals, and

2004

Stem cell studies in 2004 identify the potential to repair damaged heart tissue without having to operate.

In 2004, a promising new drug for the treatment of multiple sclerosis, Tysabri, is shown to be capable of blocking brain inflammation early in the course of the disease.

New robotics help surgeons control their hand tremors, improving the surgical outcomes for women suffering from infertility caused by fibroids, endometriosis, and congenital abnormalities.

"THERE'S ONE SHOT I ALWAYS LET THROUGH"

— CAM WARD

BLUE CROSS AND BLUE SHIELD OF NORTH CAROLINA MEMBERS... GET YOUR **FREE FLU SHOT**!

VISIT **BCBSNC.COM/FLU** FOR MORE INFORMATION AND ELIGIBILITY.

Your plan for better health.℠ | *bcbsnc.com*

 **BlueCross BlueShield of North Carolina**

Carolina Hurricanes hockey goalie Cam Ward helped BCBSNC promote flu prevention available through statewide flu shot clinics. Photo courtesy of BCBSNC archives.

BCBSNC's Centers of Excellence program recognizes top-performing specialty doctors and health care facilities that meet strict national quality standards. Photo courtesy of BCBSNC archives.

emergency medical services personnel on a new project that sought to improve the survival rate of heart attack patients.

While innovative technology and new procedures have yielded medical outcomes that previous generations could not have imagined, the pressures on physicians and hospitals also resulted in a rising number of medical errors and liability suits. In response, BCBSNC partnered with the North Carolina Hospital Association to support its Center for Hospital Quality and Patient Safety. The Center's goal of making the state's hospitals the safest in the nation by 2010 was one that BCBSNC fully endorsed through financial contributions and Bob Greczyn's participation on the Center's board.

Blue Cross and Blue Shield of North Carolina's partnerships with providers and their professional associations represented a new era in provider relations. While the hospital association was instrumental in forming BCBSNC and physicians and hospital administrators served on the Plan's board for many years, the economics of the health care industry and the changing practice of medicine altered—and sometimes strained—what was once a closer relationship. Just as BCBSNC made major changes in order

2004

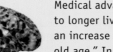

Medical advances contribute to longer lives and, with them, an increase in "diseases of old age." In 2004, Alzheimer's disease is the seventh-leading cause of death and the third-most-costly disease in the United States, after heart disease and cancer.

2005

In 2005, cancer surpasses heart disease as the leading cause of death for those under 85 years old, yet the overall cancer rate is declining due to widespread cancer screening and better cancer treatment.

In 2005, an experimental drug called GDNF is shown to reverse the loss of nerve fibers in Parkinson's disease.

to adjust to the age of managed care, physicians and hospitals did also (see *Did You Know?*). As Bob Seligson, executive vice president and CEO of the North Carolina Medical Society, explained, "It has become more difficult for doctors in a lot of areas of the state to keep their doors open because of the medical economics of running a practice."[21]

Certainly insurers, providers, regulators, and consumers all had their respective roles to play in the system of health care delivery and financing, but they also had different, sometimes diametrically opposed needs. While they sometimes found ways to collaborate positively and provide world-class health care solutions, at other times their conflicts escalated into lawsuits, misunderstood regulation, and disaffected consumers. While BCBSNC continued fiercely competing to remain the state's leading health insurer, it remained open to the needs of all of its stakeholders and kept the dialogue going during times of tension.

As it moved forward in the new millennium, BCBSNC capitalized on the advantages of being a single-state insurer. As Brad Wilson pointed out: "We know and understand North Carolina. Our market is certainly more homogeneous than it might be if we were trying to serve the country or the world. We're also fortunate that North Carolina is a growing state. The demographics indicate that after the next census we may well be the eighth-largest state in the country, surpassing New Jersey." There might also have been a regulatory upside as well, since the North

Did You Know?

Physicians and hospitals today face unprecedented economic, regulatory, and administrative pressures in running their practices and institutions.

Bob Seligson, executive vice president and CEO of the North Carolina Medical Society, acknowledged how managed care has impacted physicians: "Managed care has been a very difficult thing for doctors to deal with in North Carolina. In fact, as managed care has taken over a greater percentage of the marketplace, the difficulty of maintaining a practice has intensified. In just our office alone, we have three full-time attorneys now dealing with the regulatory aspects of the practice of medicine brought about by the increased growth of managed care entities and the need to keep up with the rules and regulations of those organizations. North Carolina is one of 19 states in which medical societies have filed class-action lawsuits against several managed care institutions because of their abusive practices, so we've tried to pursue a fairer process."[22]

Bill Pully, president of the North Carolina Hospital Association, described how hospitals struggle with payers and policymakers: "Most of the problems that hospitals face today result from rising health care costs. There's a lot of pushback from payers. I'm not talking so much about the insurance companies now as about government, Medicare and Medicaid. They are trying to reduce their exposure and their costs. Employers that have traditionally provided health insurance for their employees are also looking to reduce their costs. And often lawmakers and regulators make bad policy choices when confronted with these difficult problems. That's what we're faced with right now—an era of bad policy choices. In many cases, there are not any good choices to make, but it's a very challenging time for hospitals and people that advocate for hospitals."[23]

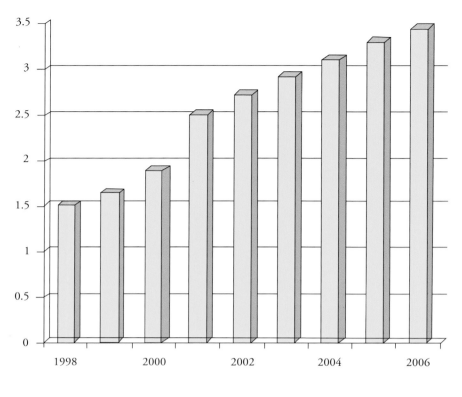

Membership Growth (in millions)

Under Bob Greczyn's leadership, BCBSNC more than doubled its membership in an eight-year period. By 2007, the Plan provided coverage for more than one in three North Carolinians. Photo courtesy of BCBSNC archives.

Carolina General Assembly knew the history of the company and its rich legacy of service to the state for 75 years. "We're in a position to have an informed conversation with the political and governmental leadership of North Carolina, to say, 'Let's think about this very, very carefully before we run off in one direction or the other under the notion of reform,'" Wilson added.[24]

In the first seven years of the twenty-first century, Blue Cross and Blue Shield of North Carolina achieved a remarkable turnaround, fine-tuning its focus on customers by offering a wide range of products, services, and information to improve their health and better address rising health care costs. As a result, membership reached an all-time high, surpassing 3.5 million members. Under Bob Greczyn's leadership, BCBSNC became a more innovative, responsive, and forward-thinking health insurer than at any other time in its history. These qualities enabled the Plan to navigate the challenges of an enormously complex, perpetually evolving health care system at both the state and national levels. At the same time, Blue Cross and Blue Shield of North Carolina remained focused on reaching those still in need of quality health care at an affordable price—just like it had in 1933.

2006

In 2006, a vaccine is approved to prevent cervical cancer.

A prescription drug benefit is added to Medicare in 2006, changing the way the federal health insurance program for elderly and disabled Americans operates.

A Look into the Future

On the eve of the Great Depression, the idea of prepayment for hospital care was born as an attempt to solve the problem of providing medical and surgical care for those who couldn't afford it. A few years later, in 1933, through the visionary pairing of a local physician and a philanthropic business leader, Durham became the home of the Hospital Care Association, the state's first hospital prepayment plan. In nearby Chapel Hill, the rival Hospital Saving Association was formed in 1935 by leaders in the university's medical school and the state medical society. These two organizations merged in 1968 to become Blue Cross and Blue Shield of North Carolina (BCBSNC), now the state's leader in delivering innovative health care products, services, and information. Membership has grown from 309 members in 1933 to more than

3.4 million members in 2007—health care insurance for approximately one out of every three North Carolinians. The founders could never have foreseen the company's remarkable growth nor envisioned customers using a computer to find a doctor or information about heart disease through BCBSNC's web site.

Yet some issues remain essentially the same as they were in 1933. There are still people in North Carolina who cannot afford to buy health insurance. There are still those who are eating unhealthy food and not getting enough exercise. While remarkable strides have been made in medical knowledge, procedures, and technology, great strides

remain to be taken in health education and controlling health care costs.

Many questions persist about the state of health delivery and financing in the nation and our state. Will people be willing to make the lifestyle changes that result in better health and lower health care costs? How much higher can health care costs climb before providers, patients, and payers revolt? Will new proposals for national health insurance surface and find greater public acceptance? Will North Carolina find ways to stem the growing number of uninsured? And will BCBSNC continue to maintain its advantages as a single-state insurer over national carriers with more market capital?

While there are no easy answers to such questions, leaders from BCBSNC, North Carolina's provider community, government, and other sectors must look actively into the future to constantly assess the opportunities and the challenges of providing health care products and services in the twenty-first century. Their thoughts provide some insight into how BCBSNC is facing the future.

On Rising Health Care Costs

Brad Wilson, BCBSNC chief operating officer:

"If you look into the crystal ball and try to say what's going to happen in 5 or 10 years, I'm not sure anyone can predict what that will be. But one thing is for certain: the pace of increase in medical expenses cannot

continue. There are going to have to be efficiencies found in the system to manage the increase or slow the pace of the increase and at the same time provide the kind of quality that all of us want when we have to access the medical system. It'll probably be a combination of private sector solution, provider community solution, and government intervention. So figuring out that equation is also one of the challenges."[1]

On Remaining Competitive

Rhone Sasser, former chairman of the BCBSNC board of trustees:

"Blue Cross and Blue Shield of North Carolina is considered the standard-bearer now. We've got a reputation for quality that gives us a tremendous advantage, but we've got to do some things to protect that name brand. So we're providing incentives to people to take more responsibility for their own health care. I think that we're setting examples in North Carolina that can be used nationwide to not only afford people better health but better health care at a more reasonable cost. So that's where we've got to go."[2]

On Provider Relations

Bob Seligson, executive vice president and CEO of the North Carolina Medical Society:

"I think what insurers could do to help improve the relationships with doctors the most is to listen. Listen to what the doctors are saying. Put themselves in their shoes so that they can understand a little bit better what impact an insurer's policies and procedures have on the day-to-day practice of medicine."[3]

Bill Pully, president of the North Carolina Hospital Association:

"We have a good culture of collaboration and cooperation between providers and payers like Blue Cross and Blue Shield of North Carolina in our state, but I think we have to continue to fight to make sure that it remains the pervasive culture for delivering health care services in North Carolina."[4]

On Customers and Employees

Bob Greczyn, president and chief executive officer of BCBSNC:

"The success of an organization is the people and the customers. We're a North Carolina company, so I look at North Carolinians as our former customers, our current customers, or our future customers. We can't make people healthier, but we can certainly be a part of the support system that allows them to choose better health. So in my view, part of being successful as a business is providing our customers a product that they want to buy, information they can use, a competitive premium, and great service. All of those things add up to the right customer experience and will allow us to keep our customers.

And we have great people that work here. You know, you can provide the motivation for people, you can provide the focus and the tools and the workplace environment, but ultimately if you don't have great people, you don't have a great company. I'm very proud of what we've been able to accomplish, and I think it's just the beginning. I think the future is brighter than today."[5]

For 75 years, BCBSNC has helped improve the health of North Carolinians. Looking ahead, the Plan brings a proud legacy of social responsibility to the state's citizens, an ability to adapt, innovate, and grow, and strong community partnerships that will continue to inform its understanding of the state's evolving and complex health care needs. BCBSNC knows that its success is tied to the success of North Carolina itself. As it has been from the beginning, Blue Cross and Blue Shield of North Carolina is committed to a healthy future for not only its members but for all North Carolinians.

Notes

**Chapter One: The Birth of the Blues
in North Carolina**

1. "Problem No. 1," *Time*, July 18, 1938.

2. James Cranford Hoyle, "The Roanoke Rapids Health Plan and the Origin of North Carolina Blue Cross," *North Carolina Medical Journal* (1971): 189.

3. "Our First Member: A Visit with Roy Medlin," *Bluebird*, August 1973, 12.

4. "Fifty and Forward," BCBSNC commemorative publication, September 1983, 5.

5. Ibid.

6. C. A. (Bill) Houck, video interview by Diana Newton, June 27, 2005, interview transcript, 2.

7. Robert C. Cunningham, III, and Robert M. Cunningham, Jr., *The Blues: A History of the Blue Cross and Blue Shield System* (Dekalb: Northern Illinois University Press), 24.

8. "Fifty and Forward," 5.

9. Houck interview, 7.

10. "Fifty and Forward," 7.

11. Fannie Lou Bingham, "Thousands Rout Fear of Hospital Bills," *Charlotte News*, February 1937.

12. E. M. Herndon, *History of the Hospital Care Association Incorporated,* Hospital Care Association publication, 33–34.

13. Cunningham and Cunningham, *The Blues,* 28.

14. Herndon, *History of the Hospital Care Association Incorporated*, 34.

15. Cunningham and Cunningham, *The Blues,* 31.

16. Herndon, *History of the Hospital Care Association Incorporated*, 30.

17. Cunningham and Cunningham, *The Blues,* 33.

18. Ibid., 44.

**Chapter Two: A Campaign for Good Health
in North Carolina**

1. Herndon, *History of the Hospital Care Association Incorporated*, 34.

2. Cunningham and Cunningham, *The Blues,* 50–52.

3. "Fifty and Forward," 9.

4. C. A. (Bill) Houck, "My Years with Blue Cross Blue Shield (1938–1979)," unpublished memoir, BCBSNC archives, 3.

5. "Then and Now," *Bluebird*, October 1969, 11.

6. Herndon, *History of the Hospital Care Association Incorporated*, 35.

7. "Whatever Happened to Polio?" Smithsonian's National Museum of American History exhibit, April 2005, http://americanhistory.si.edu/polio/americanepi/medical.htm.

8. Good Health Association brochure, 1944, 7.

9. "NewsBriefs," August 1973, 14.

10. V. K. Hart, *The History of Blue Shield in North Carolina* (Raleigh: N.C. Medical Society, 1961), 3.

11. Herndon, *History of the Hospital Care Association Incorporated*, 32.

12. Cunningham and Cunningham, *The Blues,* 51–52.

13. Ibid., 72–73.

14. Houck interview, 6.

15. Cunningham and Cunningham, *The Blues,* 82.

Chapter Three: Growing Pains

1. William G. Anlyan, MD, "The Evolution of American Medicine and the Duke Endowment Health Care (Hospital) Division Since 1924," *North*

Carolina Medical Journal 63, no. 2 (2002): 70.

2. Herndon, *History of the Hospital Care Association Incorporated*, 44.

3. "Many North Carolina Hospitals Crowded by Deluge of Patients," *Hospital News*, March 1957, 2.

4. Herndon, *History of the Hospital Care Association Incorporated*, 41.

5. "Health Service, Inc. to Aid Nation-Wide Groups," *Community Health*, September 1950, 2.

6. Herndon, *History of the Hospital Care Association Incorporated*, 40.

7. Cunningham and Cunningham, *The Blues*, 111.

8. Peter Geilich, "An Outline History of the Hospital Care Association of Durham, North Carolina from 1945 through 1958," 6, 12–13, BCBSNC archives.

9. Houck, "My Years with Blue Cross Blue Shield," 5.

10. Quoted in Cunningham and Cunningham, *The Blues*, 99.

11. U.S. Department of Health and Human Services, Centers for Medicare and Medicaid Services, "History Overview," http://www.cms.hhs.gov/about/history/corningappa.asp.

12. Hart, *The History of Blue Shield in North Carolina*, 17.

13. Anlyan, "The Evolution of American Medicine," 70.

14. Cunningham and Cunningham, *The Blues*, 111–13.

15. "The Blue Cross Story," publication of the Blue Cross Association (1972), 17.

16. "IBM Equipment Does Everything but Take Coffee Break," *Cross-Fire*, June 1959, 7.

Chapter Four: From Cooperation to Consolidation

1. Cunningham and Cunningham, *The Blues*, 126.

2. "Forand Bill Threat," *Cross-Fire*, March 1960, 3.

3. V. K. Hart, M.D., to E. M. Herndon, February 6, 1961, BCBSNC archives.

4. E. M. Herndon to V. K. Hart, M.D., February 20, 1961, BCBSNC archives.

5. "A Word From the Boss," *Cross-Fire*, September 1961.

6. Cunningham and Cunningham, *The Blues*, 138.

7. Malcolm Gladwell, "The Moral-Hazard Myth," *New Yorker*, August 29, 2005, 47.

8. Cunningham and Cunningham, *The Blues*, 141–42.

9. "Medicare to Strengthen Blue Cross," *Hospital News*, February–March 1966, 1.

10. Cunningham and Cunningham, *The Blues*, 145.

11. Herndon, *History of the Hospital Care Association Incorporated*, 51.

12. Alex McMahon, video interview by Diana Newton, June 29, 2005, interview transcript, 4.

13. "Consolidation Forms New Blue Cross Organization," *Durham Morning Herald*, January 3, 1968, sec. B, 1.

14. McMahon interview, 2–3.

15. Ibid., 3.

16. Houck, "My Years with Blue Cross Blue Shield," 7.

17. McMahon interview, 5.

18. Ibid., 4.

19. *Blue Cross Hospital News*, October 1968, 17.

20. "What Women Should Know about Football," *Bluebird*, October 1969, 14; "Keypunch Goes Indian," *Bluebird*, January 1971, 12.

21. "Blue Cross Unveils Plans for $5 Million Home Office," *Chapel Hill Weekly*, December 30, 1969, 1.

Chapter Five: New Blue, Now a Big Business

1. John Woolley and Gerhard Peters, "President Richard M. Nixon: Remarks at a Briefing on the Nation's Health System," *American Presidency Project*, http://www.presidency.ucsb.edu/ws/?pid=2121.

2. Mike Mitka, "A Quarter Century of Health Maintenance," *Journal of the American Medical Association*, 280, no. 24 (1998): 2059–60.

3. McMahon interview, 7.

4. "State Employees: Meeting Their Challenge," *Bluebird*, May 1972, 7.

5. BCBSNC 1971 Annual Report, 1.

6. Tom Rose, audio interview by Diana Newton, August 29, 2005, interview transcript, 1.

7. Cunningham and Cunningham, *The Blues*, 178–79.

8. Ibid., 180.

9. Bill Pully, interview with Diana Newton, May 15, 2006, interview transcript, 2.

10. "Fifty and Forward," 15.

11. Rose interview, 6.

12. Ibid., 4.

13. "Fifty and Forward," 18.

14. Tom Rose, interview with Diana Newton, July 31, 2006, interview notes, 1.

15. Tom Rose, telephone conversation with Diana Newton, March 30, 2006.

16. Cunningham and Cunningham, *The Blues*, 187.

17. "LRSP," *Bluebird*, July 1976, 4.

18. "Women's Lib Is the Last Thing on Their Minds," *Bluebird*, February 1975, 6.

19. "Fifty and Forward," 21–22.

20. Douglas S. Wood, "The Rise of the HMO," CNN, http://www.cnn.com/SPECIALS/2000/democracy/doctors.under.the.knife/stories/hmo.history/.

Chapter Five Inset: The Building

1. McMahon interview, 4.
2. Howard E. Covington, Jr., *Favored by Fortune: George W. Watts and the Hills of Durham* (Chapel Hill: University of North Carolina at Chapel Hill Foundation, 2004), 304.
3. "Health Care Insurance Firm Plans New Center," *Durham Sun*, December 30, 1969, 1.
4. McMahon interview, 5.
5. Covington, *Favored by Fortune*, 304.
6. "Slopes and Angles," *Bluebird*, August 1972, 14.
7. "Blue Cross, Blue Shield Is Moving," *Chapel Hill Newspaper*, June 10, 1973, 1.
8. Theodore F. Wolff, "Something for All to Share," *Christian Science Monitor*, April 1, 1980, sec. D, 2.
9. Bruce Bland, telephone interview by Diana Newton, January 30, 2006.
10. Betsy Parker, interview by Diana Newton, June 13, 2005, interview transcript, 5.
11. "Service Center Stats," *Bluebird*, January 1973, 1.
12. Parker interview, 3.
13. "A Moving Story," *Bluebird*, August 1973, 6–7.
14. "Of Ceremonious Events on D-Day," *Bluebird*, November 1973, 5.
15. Wolff, "Something for All to Share," 2.
16. Gerald White, video interview by Diana Newton, June 17, 2005, interview transcript, 4.
17. "They Say the Darnedest Things," *Bluebird*, December 1974, 15.

18. "Our Tour (de) Force," *Bluebird*, September 1969, 10.
19. "Fifty and Forward," 15.
20. White interview, 2.
21. Parker interview, 5.

Chapter Six: The Changing Health Care Landscape

1. Judith Feder et al., eds., *National Health Insurance: Conflicting Goals and Policy Choices* (Washington, D.C.: Urban Institute, 1979), 12.
2. Fred R. Darkis, *Durham, North Carolina: City of Medicine USA* (Durham, N.C.: Self-published, 1991), 59–61.
3. Paul Starr, *The Social Transformation of American Medicine* (New York: Basic Books, 1982), 415.
4. "Big Business — Big Transformation: Health Care Trends in the Southeast," *EconSouth* (Third Quarter 2000), http://www.frbatlanta.org/invoke.cfm?objectid=87B68035–6666–11D5–93390020352A7A95&method=display.
5. BCBSNC 1982 Annual Report, 1, 7.
6. Rose interview, 7.
7. Starr, *The Social Transformation of American Medicine*, 419.
8. Rose interview, 5.
9. Ibid.
10. "Background Information: NC HMOS," North Carolina Institute of Medicine, http://www.nciom.org/hmoconguide/BCBS.html.
11. Dr. Don Bradley, interview by Diana Newton, April 25, 2006, interview transcript, 1.
12. Ibid., 2.
13. "Sixty . . . and Never Been Sick a Day in Our Life," BCBSNC commemorative publication, 1993, 17.
14. Ibid., 8.

15. Cunningham and Cunningham, *The Blues*, 209.
16. Valerie Carter, video interview by Diana Newton, April 25, 2006, interview transcript, 2.
17. Ibid., 2–3.
18. Rose interview, 12.
19. "HMO Mergers Cut Premiums in Only Most Combative Markets," Robert Woods Johnson Grant Report, 2001, http://www.rwjf.org/reports/grr/023271.htm.
20. Bradley interview, 2.
21. Rose interview, 5.
22. Bradley interview, 3.
23. Cunningham and Cunningham, *The Blues*, 215–16.
24. Rose interview, 9.

Chapter Seven: Health Care in Crisis

1. Cunningham and Cunningham, *The Blues*, 222–29.
2. "National Health Expenditures, 1960–2004," Centers for Medicare & Medicaid Services, Data from the National Health Statistics Group, http://www.cms.hhs.gov/NationalHealthExpendData/.
3. Paul Starr, "What Happened to Health Care Reform?" *American Prospect,* no. 20 (Winter 1995): 20–31.
4. Ken Otis, telephone interview by Diana Newton, August 14, 2006, interview transcript, 1.
5. Ibid.
6. "A Conversation with Ken Otis, President Elect," video interview by Kathy Higgins, 1993.
7. Starr, "What Happened to Health Care Reform?" 3.
8. Otis interview (2006), 2.

9. "A Conversation with Ken Otis," 1.

10. Wilson interview, 6.

11. Joseph Goedert, "HIPAA's Long and Winding Road," *Health Data Management*, February 2003, 6.

12. Harry Reynolds, video interview by Diana Newton, May 16, 2006, interview transcript, 5.

13. Ibid.

14. Bob Greczyn, video interview by Judy van Wyk, June 27, 2006, interview transcript, 6.

15. Otis interview (2006), 3.

16. Brad Adcock, interview by Diana Newton, August 21, 2006, interview transcript, 1.

17. Ibid.

18. North Carolina G.S. § 58-65-131.

19. Ibid.; North Carolina G.S. § 58-65-132; North Carolina G.S. § 58-65-133.

20. Adcock interview, 3.

21. "North Carolina BCBS Update," Community Health Assets Project, http://www.consumersunion.org/conv/pub/statencstates/000621.html.

22. Bradley interview, 6.

23. Carter interview, 4.

24. Ken Lerner, video interview by Diana Newton, May 16, 2006, interview transcript, 4.

25. "Patient Rights and Responsibilities," Consumer.gov, http://www.consumer.gov/qualityhealth/rights.htm.

26. Governor James B. (Jim) Hunt, video interview by Judy van Wyk, May 24, 2006, interview transcript, 2.

27. Otis interview (2006), 4.

Chapter Eight: A New Blue for the New Millennium

1. "Y2K: Overhyped and Oversold?" BBC News Talking Point, January 6, 2000, http://news.bbc.co.uk/2/hi/talking_point/586938.stm.

2. "Executive Profile: Always on the Ball," *North Carolina*, March 2005, 62.

3. Greczyn interview, 2.

4. Kathy Higgins, video interview by Diana Newton, May 16, 2006, 1.

5. Ibid., 2.

6. Hunt interview, 2.

7. Aaron McKethan, "The Problem of Uninsurance in North Carolina," Institute for Emerging Issues Briefing Notes, 2005, 1.

8. North Carolina G. S. § 58-65-133.

9. Higgins interview, 6.

10. Bonnie Eksten, "State Scrutinizes Blue Cross Switch," *Morning Star* (Wilmington, N.C.), January 12, 2002, sec. C, 8.

11. Ned Cline, "Conversion Foes: It's Our Blue Cross to Bear," *Business, North Carolina*, October 1, 2003, 24.

12. Brad Wilson, interview by Diana Newton, June 7, 2006, interview transcript, 7.

13. Greczyn interview, 5.

14. Ibid.

15. Rhone Sasser, interview by Diana Newton, July 26, 2006, interview transcript, 5.

16. Mike Frazier, "Insurers Tackle Obesity Head On," *Advertising Age* (Midwest region edition), February 7, 2005, 3.

17. Phil Galewizt, "North Carolina Leads the Way in Free Health Care," *Knight Ridder Tribune Business News*, February 20, 2005, 1.

18. NCAFC 2005 Annual Report, 2.

19. Mike Darrow, e-mail message to author, December 15, 2006.

20. Jean P. Fisher, "Program to Sustain Rural Health Care," *News and Observer*, February 22, 2006.

21. Bob Seligson, video interview by Diana Newton, June 6, 2006, interview transcript, 1.

22. Ibid., 2.

23. Pully interview, 1.

24. Wilson interview, 3.

Conclusion: A Look into the Future

1. Wilson interview, 3.

2. Sasser interview, 7.

3. Seligson interview, 7.

4. Pully interview, 5.

5. Greczyn interview, 7.